Simply Wonderful Recipes

ERIC THEISS

Acknowledgments

I feel incredibly lucky to have had so many talented people help me to bring this book to fruition. I depend on Claire Winslow not only for her vast culinary knowledge and attention to detail but also for her ability to keep me on task. I would also like to acknowledge the hard work put in by her team, including Andrew Bergman and Ed Buldowski. Thank you to Jeanette Mostowicz for her food styling contributions and ability to put up with me. Thanks to Skippy Sicari for his numerous contributions as the Prime Minister of Props and as my stunt double!

For making the book look beautiful with its art and design, I would be remiss if I didn't thank Parker Bliss and Daniel Suquitana. To my photographer Matt Wagemann and his assistant Mike Livi, thank you for getting great shots of me despite my lack of modeling skills and for making the food pop off of the page so well. I want to thank Zachary Bridge for his editing work on this book. Also, big thanks to Pete Calciano for bringing all of these talented people together and for being so accommodating.

Lastly, I would like to thank Elizabeth Jones and Joann Herrera for powdering, poking, and prodding until I look good enough for the camera. Now THAT takes a village.

Eric Theiss

Table of Contents

Bread & Breakfast

Sandwiches

Poultry

Soups & Stews

Veggies & Potatoes

Fish & Seafood

Meats

One-Pot Meals & Casseroles

Desserts

About the Author

Eric Theiss's culinary savoir-faire started in northern NJ when his Italian mother, sensing a talent for cooking in six-year-old Eric, borrowed the first cookbook he would ever use from the public library. Her intuition was correct, and Eric began a life of culinary work. As a young adult, he continued to fuel his passion for food and fine dining. During his early 20s, this passion manifested itself in the long nights Eric spent working in NJ restaurants, including his favorite kitchen at The Culinary Renaissance, where acclaimed chef Frank Falcinelli (owner of NY coffee shop Cafe Pedlar and restaurants Frankies 457 Spuntino, Frankies 570 Spuntino, and Prime Meats) exposed Eric to a level of culinary excellence that inspired Eric to strive. In 1997, Eric took a leap of faith and opened his own fine dining restaurant and bar in West Chester, PA called Meritage, which enjoyed rave reviews from some prominent Philadelphia food critics. With Meritage, his dream of owning and operating a fine dining establishment was fully realized.

A few years later, utilizing his inventive and creative flair, Eric moved on to the culinary broadcast world, working in product development for not only QVC's proprietary kitchenware lines but also celebrity lines (Paula Deen, Emeril, Rocco, Rachael Ray, and Lidia Bastianich) and his own personal line of kitchen tools and cookware.

Eric has been a popular TV chef presenter for over 15 years on QVC's live shows, promoting both his own brands and a variety of well-known national kitchen brands. In addition, Eric owns and operates a company that brokers many new and innovative products for QVC. His most recent business venture, a successful new publishing company, publishes and distributes cookbooks and pamphlets nationwide.

Paramount to his career thus far, Eric currently hosts several incredibly successful, award-winning infomercials featuring the Power Pressure Cooker XL, the Power Air Fryer Oven, and Copper Chef, each of which has sold millions of units and has achieved a TOP 5 status. Eric wrote this cookbook to complement his newest infomercial, the Wonder Cooker, which helps people save time, storage, and money because of its incredible multi-functionality.

Eric currently lives near the live studios at QVC in PA along with his wife, Jessica, and his two sons, Cameron and Maxwell.

Questions & Answers

1. **How many different kitchen pans & appliances does the Wonder Cooker replace?**

   The Wonder Cooker is a 14-in-1 multi-use cooker. It replaces your deep roaster, shallow roaster, dual roaster, Dutch oven, stock pot, grill pan, steamer, skillet, baking dish, deep fryer, slow cooker, chafing dish, casserole dish, and indoor grill.

2. **Do I need to use any butter or oil?**

   The Wonder Cooker is designed with Advanced Cerami-Tech Non-Stick Coating. There's no need to add any extra butter, grease, or oil.

3. **Is there a coating on the Wonder Cooker that burns off at first use?**

   No. As with all cookware, remember to wash with nonabrasive soap before first use.

4. **What is the Wonder Cooker made of?**

   The Wonder Cooker is constructed of highest quality, thick cast aluminum with Cerami-Tech Non-Stick Coating. You get built-in, stainless steel induction plates on both the bottom of the Roaster Pan as well as the Lid (Grill Pan).

5. **How do I clean my Wonder Cooker?**

   We recommend you clean the Wonder Cooker's components by hand with water, a mild soap or cleanser, and a soft, nonmetallic scrubber, sponge, or bristle brush. Or, you may put them in the dishwasher.

6. **Is the Wonder Cooker designed to go in the oven?**

   The Wonder Cooker is designed for any stovetop— including induction—while 850° F heat resistance makes it equally perfect for the oven.

7. **Does the Wonder Cooker contain PTFE or PFOA?**

   Absolutely not. The Wonder Cooker is free of both PTFE & PFOA.

8. **What kind of utensils should I use with the Wonder Cooker?**

   We recommend you use only nonmetallic utensils made of wood, plastic, silicone, or bamboo.

9. **How do I store the Wonder Cooker?**

   To protect the surface of the Wonder Cooker, we do not recommend stacking other cookware inside of the pans during storage. Use a soft cloth to protect the coating if you must store the Wonder Cooker with other cookware.

10. **Are there any special safety precautions I should follow?**

    Always remember to use potholders, as the handles and lid can get hot when on the stovetop and in the oven. When lifting the lid, divert your face and body from the Wonder Cooker as hot steam may escape.

Why Wonder Cooker?

My entire professional life, I have been interested in helping customers pare down their crowded kitchen drawers and cabinets by bringing them items with multiple functions. Never has this been more apparent than with my newest product, the Copper Chef Wonder Cooker!

This looks like a traditional roasting pan at first, but it is so much more than that. The Copper Chef Wonder Cooker features an innovative two-piece design; the base is a deep roaster and the lid is a shallow roaster with grill grates. This means that you can cook in them separately, together with the lid on, or you can even stack them! While it will be your best roaster ever with its amazing chemical-free Cerami-Tech Non-Stick Coating, which makes clean up a joke, this pan set also performs several other jobs in your kitchen!

An unbelievably useful two-piece set, the Copper Chef Wonder Cooker performs many different cooking functions for you. It acts as an XL deep roaster (9-L capacity), and it also acts as a shallow roaster (the lid itself), stock pot, grill pan, baking pan, casserole, deep fryer, steamer, slow cooker, Dutch oven, chafing dish, and electric grill (when you use it on the Copper Chef Induction Cooktop, which is sold separately).

The Wonder Cooker is not only super useful but also extremely well made. We used thick cast aluminum, which means its very durable but also lightweight, something that I know many of my customers prefer. It features a stainless steel induction plate, so you can use it on any type of cooking surface (gas, electric, or induction). We made sure it is chemical PTFE and PFOA free and can withstand heat up to 850° F! What makes it even better? It's dishwasher safe. I hope you enjoy your Copper Chef Wonder Cooker and that it allows you to simplify your kitchen.

Equivalency Charts

Dry (Weight) Measurements

Misc.*	Teaspoons	Tablespoons	Ounces	Cups	Grams	Pounds
1 dash	$1/16$ tsp.	-	-	-	-	-
1 pinch/6 drops	$1/8$ tsp.	-	-	-	-	-
15 drops	¼ tsp.	-	-	-	-	-
1 splash	½ tsp.	-	-	-	-	-
-	1 tsp.	$1/3$ tbsp.	$1/6$ oz	-	-	-
-	3 tsp.	1 tbsp.	½ oz	-	14.3 g	-
-	-	2 tbsp.	1 oz	$1/8$ cup	28.3 g	-
-	-	4 tbsp.	2 oz	¼ cup	56.7 g	-
-	-	5 $1/3$ tbsp.	2.6 oz	$1/3$ cup	75.6 g	-
-	-	8 tbsp.	4 oz	½ cup	113.4 g	-
-	-	12 tbsp.	6 oz	¾ cup	170.1 g	-
-	-	16 tbsp.	8 oz	1 cup	226.8 g	½ lb
-	-	32 tbsp.	16 oz	2 cups	453.6 g	1 lb
-	-	64 tbsp.	32 oz	4 cups/1 qt.	907.2 g	2 lb

* Dash, pinch, drop, and splash are subjective measurements that have no formally agreed-upon definition.

Abbreviations

Term	Dry & Liquid	Abbreviation
cup	usually liquid	-
fluid ounce	only liquid	fl oz.
gallon	dry or liquid	-
inch	-	in.
ounce	dry	oz.
pint	dry or liquid	-
pound	dry	lb
quart	dry or liquid	qt./qts.
teaspoon	dry or liquid	tsp.
tablespoon	dry or liquid	tbsp.

Liquid (Volume) Measurements

Fluid Ounces	Tablespoons	Cups	Milliliter/Liters	Pints	Quarts	Gallons
1 fl oz	2 tbsp.	1/8 cup	30 ml	-	-	-
2 fl oz	4 tbsp.	1/4 cup	60 ml	-	-	-
4 fl oz	8 tbsp.	1/2 cup	125 ml	-	-	-
8 fl oz	16 tbsp.	1 cup	250 ml	-	-	-
12 fl oz	-	1 1/2 cups	375 ml	-	-	-
16 fl oz	-	2 cups	500 ml	1 pint	-	-
32 fl oz	-	4 cups	1 L	2 pints	1 qt.	-
128 fl oz	-	16 cups	4 L	8 pints	4 qts.	1 gallon

Cooking Temperature Charts

Safe steps in food handling, cooking, and storage are essential for preventing foodborne illness. You can't see, smell, or taste harmful bacteria that may cause illness.

Cook all food to these minimum internal temperatures as measured with a food thermometer before removing food from the heat source. Let rest for a minimum of 10 mins. before serving unless indicated otherwise.

In every step of food preparation, follow the four guidelines to help keep food safe:

Clean—*Wash hands and surfaces often.*
Separate—*Separate raw meat from other foods.*
Cook—*Cook to the right temperature.*
Chill—*Refrigerate food promptly.*

Doneness	Serving Temperature	Serving Temperature
	Eric's Recommendation	USDA's Recommendation
Beef, Lamb, Pork, Veal Steaks, Chops & Roasts		
Rare	125° F (52° C)	*
Medium Rare	130° F (54° C)	*
Medium	135° F (57° C)	
Medium Well	150° F (65° C)	Minimum Internal Temperature & Rest Time: 145° F (63° C) and allow to rest for at least 3 mins.*
Well Done	Over 150° F (over 65° C)	

Doneness	Serving Temperature	Serving Temperature
	Eric's Recommendation	**USDA's Recommendation**
Ground Meats, Burgers, Meatloaf & Sausages Except Poultry		
Recommended	160° F (71° C)	Minimum Internal Temperature: 160° F (71° C)*
Burgers (Beef)		
Recommended	140° F (60° C)	160° F (71° C)
Pork Ribs, Pork Shoulders		
Tender and Juicy	180-190° F (82–88° C)	*
Precooked Ham		
Recommended	140° F (60° C)	Reheat cooked hams packaged in USDA-inspected plants to 140° F (60° C); all others to 165° F (74° C)*
Turkey & Chicken, Whole or Ground		
Recommended	165° F (74° C)	Minimum Internal Temperature: 165° F (74° C)*
Fish		
Rare	125° F (52° C)	*
Medium	135° F (57° C)	*
Well Done	145° F (63° C)	Minimum Internal Temperature: 145° F (63° C)*
Unpasteurized Eggs		
Recommended	160° F (71° C)	Minimum Internal Temperature: 160° F (71° C)*

*Consuming raw or undercooked meats, poultry, seafood, shellfish, or eggs may increase your risk of foodborne illness.
  http://fsis.usda.gov/

BREAD & BREAKFAST

Apple Cider Doughnuts

Crustless Chorizo Quiche

Ham, Spinach & Caramelized Onion Frittata

Ginger & Dried Cherry Sticky Buns

Garlic & Sun-Dried Tomato Dinner Rolls

Savory Cornbread

Bacon Buttermilk Biscuits

Dutch Oven Bread

Pecan Butterscotch Coffee Cakes

French Toast with Pecan Compound Butter

Strawberry Mascarpone-Stuffed French Toast

Garlic, Lemon & Thyme Focaccia

Apple Cider Doughnuts

SERVES 13

Ingredients

2 cups apple cider

3 ½ cups flour

⅔ cup brown sugar

2 tsp. baking powder

¾ tsp. salt

½ tsp. baking soda

¼ tsp. cinnamon

¼ tsp. grated nutmeg

½ tsp. lemon zest

2 eggs

6 tbsp. butter, melted & cooled

Cinnamon–Sugar Topping

¾ cup sugar

2 tbsp. cinnamon

———

5 qts. canola oil

Directions

1. Place a pot on the stove top. Bring the apple cider to a boil over high heat and reduce by half. Let cool.

2. Combine the flour, brown sugar, baking powder, salt, baking soda, cinnamon, nutmeg, and lemon zest in a bowl to make the dry mixture.

3. Add the eggs, cooled cider, and melted butter to a separate bowl and mix to make the wet mixture.

4. Pour the wet mixture into the dry mixture and mix until dough is formed. Let rest for 1 hr. at room temperature.

5. Add the cinnamon–sugar topping ingredients to a separate bowl and whisk together. Reserve the topping in the bowl.

6. Place the Wonder Cooker's Roaster Pan on the stove top. Heat the canola oil over medium-high heat until the temperature reaches 325° F/160° C.

7. Roll the dough into a ½ in.-thick rectangle on a floured surface.

8. Cut nine doughnuts and doughnut holes using a 3-in. doughnut cutter. Reroll the extra dough and cut four more doughnuts from it.

9. Deep fry the doughnuts in the Roaster Pan until golden brown (about 1 ½ mins.).

10. Place the doughnuts on a cooling rack to drain and cool.

11. Toss the doughnuts in the cinnamon–sugar topping before serving.

Eric's Tip: Day-old apple cider doughnuts make the *best* bread pudding!

Crustless Chorizo Quiche

SERVES 8–12

Ingredients

2 poblano peppers, diced finely

1 tbsp. olive oil

12 oz chorizo, skin removed

1 medium Spanish onion, diced

12 eggs

¾ cup milk

1 ½ cups heavy cream

1 tbsp. butter, melted

1 tsp. cumin

2 tsp. paprika

1 tsp. salt

½ tsp. ground black pepper

8 oz Monterey Jack cheese

Directions

1. Place the poblano peppers on the Wonder Cooker's Grill Pan. Place in the oven and broil until the poblano peppers are blackened.

2. Peel and dice the poblano peppers.

3. Preheat the oven to 350° F/175° C.

4. Place the Roaster Pan on the stove top. Heat the olive oil over medium heat, cook the chorizo for 4–5 mins., and then add the onion.

5. Combine the eggs, milk, cream, butter, cumin, paprika, salt, and ground black pepper in a bowl to make the egg batter.

6. Layer the chorizo and onions on the bottom of the Grill Pan, top with the poblano peppers and cheese, and pour the egg batter over the top.

7. Place the Grill Pan in the oven and bake at 350° F/175° C until set (30–45 mins.).

Eric's Tip: If you can't find fresh chorizo, just mix together 12 oz ground pork, 3 tbsp. paprika, and 2 tbsp. freshly chopped garlic.

Ham, Spinach & Caramelized Onion Frittata

Ingredients

4 tbsp. butter, melted, divided

1 onion, sliced thinly

40 eggs

1 ¼ cups heavy cream

2 tbsp. flour

½ tsp. salt

½ tsp. ground black pepper

¼ tsp. ground cayenne pepper

2 lb tater tots

14 oz ham, diced

3 cups spinach, chopped

14 oz fontina cheese, grated

Directions

1. Preheat the oven to 350° F/175° C.

2. Place the Wonder Cooker's Roaster Pan on the stove top. Melt 1 tbsp. butter over medium-high heat and then sauté the onions until brown. Remove and reserve the onions.

3. Add the eggs, heavy cream, flour, salt, ground black pepper, ground cayenne pepper, and 3 tbsp. melted butter to a bowl and whisk together to make the egg mixture.

4. Layer the tater tots in the bottom of the Roaster Pan and then top with the ham, spinach, and fontina cheese.

5. Pour the egg mixture into the Roaster Pan and sprinkle the onions over the top.

6. Place the Roaster Pan in the oven and bake at 350° F/175° C for 1–1 ¼ hrs.

Eric's Tip: Caramelizing the onion will not only give a great depth of flavor but also prevent the frittata from getting watered down when the onions cook.

Ginger & Dried Cherry Sticky Buns

SERVES 16

Ingredients

1 stick butter

1 cup brown sugar

¾ cup heavy cream

2 tbsp. honey

zest of ½ orange

1 tbsp. sugar

1 tsp. ground cinnamon

3 tubes refrigerated crescent roll dough

1 ½ cups dried cherries

1 egg, whisked

Glaze

3 tbsp. orange juice

1 tbsp. milk

2 tsp. grated ginger

___

¼ cup chopped candied ginger

Directions

1. Preheat the oven to 350° F/175° C.

2. Place a saucepan on the stove top. Melt the butter over medium-high heat and then stir in the brown sugar, cream, honey, and orange zest to make the sugar mixture.

3. Raise the heat to bring the mixture to a boil and then reduce the heat to simmer for 3 mins.

4. Combine the sugar and cinnamon in a small bowl and mix.

5. Roll the crescent roll dough into a ¼ in.-thick rectangle. Sprinkle the cinnamon and sugar mix in an even layer over the dough and top with the dried cherries, leaving a 1-in. strip clear along the top side of the dough.

6. Brush the strip with the whisked egg and then tightly roll the dough from the bottom toward the top to form a log.

7. Pour the sugar mixture into the Wonder Cooker's Grill Pan.

8. Cut the dough log into 16 even pieces and line the Grill Pan with the pieces, cut side down, in even rows. Brush with the whisked egg.

9. Place the Grill Pan in the oven and bake at 350° F/175° C for 40 mins. Remove the buns from the oven and let cool for 5 mins.

10. Brush the buns with the remaining sugar mixture from the saucepan.

11. Combine the glaze ingredients in a separate bowl and then drizzle over the top of the buns.

12. Top with the candied ginger.

Eric's Tip: I love taking day-old sticky buns, slicing them in half, and cooking them French toast style for an awesome brunch treat.

Garlic & Sun-Dried Tomato Dinner Rolls

Ingredients

2 ¼-oz packets active dry yeast

½ cup water

2 cups milk

⅔ cup sugar

1 ½ sticks butter, melted

9 ½ cups flour

5 eggs

2 tsp. salt

1 3-oz bag sun-dried tomatoes, diced finely

Topping

2 sticks butter

6 cloves garlic, minced

Directions

1. Add the yeast and water to a mixer bowl. Reserve the yeast in the mixer bowl.

2. Add the milk, sugar, and 1 ½ sticks melted butter in a separate bowl to make the milk mixture. Let cool.

3. Pour the flour and sun-dried tomatoes into the mixer bowl with the yeast.

4. Pour in the milk mixture and mix.

5. Mix in the eggs in one at a time and then mix in the salt until the dough is mixed.

6. Cover the dough and reserve in a warm area. Let rise until the dough doubles in size (about 1 hr.).

7. Divide the dough into 30 pieces and roll each piece into a ball.

8. Divide the dough balls evenly between the Wonder Cooker's Grill Pan and the Roaster Pan.

9. Cover loosely with plastic and let rise again in a warm area (about 30 mins.).

10. Preheat the oven to 350° F/175° C.

11. Place both Pans in the oven and cook at 350° F/175° C until lightly golden.

12. Place a saucepot on the oven. Melt the garlic and butter over medium-high heat until the butter is toasted.

13. Pour the butter over the rolls before serving.

Eric's Tip: I love to pair these rolls with my Nonna's meatballs for Italian sliders – just add sharp provolone.

Savory Cornbread

Ingredients

3 cups flour

2 cups yellow cornmeal

2 tbsp. baking powder

2 tsp. salt

2 tsp. chipotle powder

5 tbsp. sugar

1 tbsp. chopped thyme

4 eggs

2 ½ cups milk

2 sticks butter, melted

2 cups frozen corn

2 cups shredded cheddar cheese

Directions

1. Preheat the oven to 400° F/205° C.

2. Add the flour, cornmeal, baking powder, salt, chipotle powder, sugar, and thyme to a bowl and whisk to combine to make the dry mixture.

3. Add the eggs, milk, and melted butter to a separate bowl and whisk to combine to make the wet mixture.

4. Pour the wet mixture into the dry mixture and stir to make the batter.

5. Stir in the corn and cheddar cheese.

6. Pour the batter into the Wonder Cooker's Grill Pan.

7. Place the Grill Pan in the oven and bake at 400° F/205° C for 30 mins.

Eric's Tip: This recipe is so good that I will make it specifically for my famous holiday cornbread stuffing.

Bacon Buttermilk Biscuits

SERVES 12

Ingredients

3 ¾ cups flour

1 ½ tbsp. baking powder

1 ½ tsp. baking soda

1 ¼ tsp. salt

6 thick slices bacon, cooked
& cut into ½-in. pieces

1 stick butter, cold & cubed

1 ¾ cups buttermilk

3 tbsp. butter, melted

maple syrup, for serving

Directions

1. Preheat the oven to 450° F/230° C.

2. Whisk together the flour, baking powder, baking soda, and salt in a bowl.

3. Mix with the bacon pieces and cubed butter in a food processor until pea-sized lumps are formed.

4. Pour in the buttermilk and mix until a dough just comes together.

5. Roll the dough out into a ½ in.-thick rectangle on a floured surface. Cut into 12 pieces with a cookie cutter. Evenly space the pieces on the Wonder Cooker's Grill Pan.

6. Place the Grill Pan in the oven and bake at 450° F/230° C until golden brown (20–25 mins.).

7. Brush the biscuits with the melted butter while still hot and serve with maple syrup.

Eric's Tip: My favorite Southern treat is fresh biscuits, baked ham, and pepper jelly.

Dutch Oven Bread

MAKES 1 LOAF

Ingredients

6 cups all-purpose flour, plus more for handling dough

1 tbsp. salt

2 tsp. active dry yeast

2 tbsp. sugar

3 cups water, warm

Directions

1. Combine the flour, salt, yeast, and sugar in a bowl and whisk well.

2. Add the water to the bowl and mix until fully absorbed. The dough will be sticky.

3. Cover the bowl with plastic wrap and let proof at room temperature for at least 12 hrs. (up to 24 hrs.).

4. When ready to bake, preheat the oven to 450° F/230° C.

5. Place the Wonder Cooker in the oven for 30 mins.

6. While the Wonder Cooker heats up in the oven, turn out the dough onto a counter that has been generously coated with flour.

7. Flatten the dough into a rectangle. Roll the dough, long ways, by hand to form a log. Tuck the edges and shape the dough into an oval loaf.

8. Carefully remove the Wonder Cooker from the oven.

9. Place the loaf onto the Grill Pan and cover with the Roaster Pan to form the Dutch Oven.

10. Place the Dutch Oven in the oven and bake at 450° F/230° C for 45 mins.

11. Remove the Roaster Pan and bake at 450° F/230° C for an additional 15 mins.

12. Cool before serving.

Eric's Tip: This bread recipe is all purpose. You can roll brown sugar, cinnamon, and raisins for a sweet treat or roll sliced pepperoni and provolone to go with your spaghetti and meatballs.

Pecan Butterscotch Coffee Cakes

Ingredients

Pecan Crumb Topping

1 cup chopped pecans

1 ¼ cups brown sugar

½ cup butter, softened

———

2 sticks butter, softened

1 cup sugar

1 cup brown sugar

4 eggs

2 cups buttermilk, room temperature

5 cups flour

1 tbsp. baking powder

1 tsp. salt

Caramel Sauce

2 cups sugar

⅔ cup water

½ stick butter

1 ½ cups heavy cream

1 tsp. vanilla extract

Directions

1. Preheat the oven to 350° F/175° C.

2. Combine the pecan crumb topping ingredients in a small bowl by hand until crumbly. Reserve the topping in the bowl.

3. Combine the butter and sugar in an electric mixer and mix until light and fluffy.

4. Add the eggs one at a time, scraping down the bowl after each addition.

5. Gradually add the buttermilk.

6. Add in the flour, baking soda, and salt and mix until just combined.

7. Pour into the Wonder Cooker's Roaster Pan and sprinkle with the pecan crumb topping.

8. Place the Roaster Pan in the oven and cook at 350° F/175° C until a toothpick inserted into the center comes out clean (45–50 mins.).

9. Place a saucepan on the stove top. Bring the sugar and water to a boil over high heat to make the caramel sauce. Once the sauce takes on a caramel color, add the butter and slowly add in the cream (the sauce will foam up in the saucepan).

10. Once combined, add in the vanilla extract.

11. Serve the finished coffee cake with the caramel sauce.

Eric's Tip: Turn these delicious coffee cakes into a decadent dessert by placing a scoop of French vanilla ice cream for an ala mode delight!

French Toast
with Pecan Compound Butter

Ingredients

Compound Butter

2 sticks butter

2 tbsp. brown sugar

½ tsp. cinnamon

2 tbsp. ground pecans

¼ cup chopped pecans

———

6 eggs

1 cup half and half

½ cup heavy cream

1 tsp. orange zest

½ tsp. vanilla extract

1 tsp. cinnamon

½ fresh nutmeg, grated

½ tsp. salt

1 tbsp. sugar

1 tbsp. butter

1 loaf challah bread, sliced thickly

Directions

1. Combine the compound butter ingredients in a bowl, roll into a log, and freeze.

2. Combine the eggs, half and half, cream, orange zest, vanilla extract, cinnamon, nutmeg, salt, and sugar in a separate bowl to make the egg mixture.

3. Place the Wonder Cooker's Roaster Pan on the stove top. Melt the butter over medium heat.

4. Dip the bread into the egg mixture, place in the Roaster Pan, and fry each side until golden brown.

5. Serve with slices of the compound butter.

Eric's Tip: Compound butter is a blank canvas for any flavor you wish. I'll leave out the pecans and mix in orange zest and a small pinch of fresh chopped thyme. Grated dark chocolate and ground hazelnuts are another favorite of mine.

SERVES 4

Strawberry Mascarpone-Stuffed
French Toast

Ingredients

5 qts. canola oil

3 eggs

½ cup heavy cream

½ cup sugar

1 ½ tsp. cinnamon

1 ½ tsp. vanilla extract

1 cup flour

4 tbsp. mascarpone

4 tbsp. cream cheese

8 slices white bread

8 tbsp. strawberry jam

powdered sugar, for serving

Directions

1. Place the Wonder Cooker's Roaster Pan on the stove top. Heat the canola oil over medium-high heat until the temperature reaches 325° F/160° C.

2. Whisk together the eggs, cream, sugar, cinnamon, vanilla, and flour in a large bowl to make the egg mixture. Reserve the egg mixture in the bowl.

3. Combine the mascarpone and cream cheese in a separate small bowl and mix to make the cheese mixture.

4. Spread the cheese mixture on 4 bread slices.

5. Spread the strawberry jam on the remaining 4 bread slices and then sandwich them on top of the cheese-covered slices, jelly side down.

6. Cut each sandwich into four triangular pieces.

7. Dip the triangles in the egg mixture and then deep fry until golden brown (2–3 mins.).

8. Serve with a dusting of powdered sugar.

Eric's Tip: If mascarpone cheese is not available, you can mix regular cream cheese with a little sour cream.

Garlic, Lemon & Thyme Focaccia

SERVES 10–12

Ingredients

2 16-oz bags pre-prepared pizza dough

2 tbsp. olive oil

6 cloves garlic, sliced

4–5 large sprigs thyme

zest of 1 lemon

Directions

1. Preheat the oven to 400° F/205° C.

2. Work the dough into the bottom of the Wonder Cooker's Grill Pan.

3. Make evenly spaced indents in the top of the dough with the tips of your fingers.

4. Drizzle the olive oil over the top of the dough.

5. Sprinkle the surface of the dough with the garlic and thyme.

6. Place the Grill Pan in the oven and bake at 400° F/205° C until golden brown (35–40 mins.).

7. Sprinkle with the lemon zest before serving.

Eric's Tip: I love making breakfast sandwiches with this focaccia bread: fried egg, crispy bacon, baby arugula, and fontina cheese!

SANDWICHES

Chipotle Chicken, Bacon & Ranch Panini

Pulled Chicken Panini

Hot Roast Beef Panini

Muffaletta Panini

Pastrami Coleslaw Panini

Braised Beef Grilled Cheese

Guacamole Grilled Cheese

Pizza Grilled Cheese

Monte Cristo

Taco Sliders

Chicken Cordon Bleu Sliders

Potato- & Bacon-Stuffed Hamburgers

Italian Sausage & Pepper Sliders

Chipotle Chicken, Bacon &
Ranch Panini

SERVES 4

Ingredients

4 chicken breasts

½ tsp. salt

½ tsp. ground black pepper

1 tbsp. ground chipotle pepper

4 tbsp. ranch dressing

4 club rolls, cut in half

8 slices Monterey Jack cheese

8 slices bacon, cooked

½ cup margarine

Directions

1. Season the chicken with the salt, ground black pepper, and ground chipotle pepper.

2. Place the Wonder Cooker's Grill Pan on a grill. Preheat the grill.

3. Grill the chicken in the Grill Pan.

4. Spread 1 tbsp. ranch dressing on the cut side of each roll half.

5. Lay 1 Monterey Jack cheese slice on the ranch dressing on each roll half.

6. Lay 1 chicken breast on each roll's bottom half.

7. Top each chicken breast with 2 bacon slices.

8. Cover each roll's bottom half with the top half, cheese side down.

9. Butter and then grill each side of the paninis over medium heat until the cheese is melted and the bread is golden brown.

Eric's Tip: Sometimes, if I'm in a beach mood, I'll grill fresh mahi mahi instead of the chicken breast.

Pulled Chicken Panini

SERVES 4

Ingredients

10 oz cooked chicken, shredded

1 cup BBQ sauce

4 round rolls, cut in half

8 slices cheddar cheese

½ cup margarine

Directions

1. Combine the chicken and BBQ sauce in a bowl and mix.

2. Scoop 1 tbsp. bread out of the cut side of the rolls' top halves.

3. Lay 1 cheddar cheese slice on the cut side of each roll half.

4. Scoop the chicken mixture onto each roll's bottom half and then cover with the roll's top half.

5. Place the Wonder Cooker's Grill Pan on the stove top. Butter and then grill each side of the sandwiches over medium heat until the cheese is melted and the bread is golden brown.

Eric's Tip: Sometimes, when I'm feeling saucy, I'll substitute the BBQ sauce with either buffalo sauce or Korean gochujang.

Hot Roast Beef Panini

SERVES 2

Ingredients

Gravy Mixture

2 tbsp. olive oil

1 garlic clove, crushed

4 oz onions

2 button mushrooms

4 tbsp. gravy

———

4 slices Swiss cheese

4 slices oval bread

½ lb roast beef

¼ cup margarine

Directions

1. Place the Wonder Cooker's Roaster Pan on the stove top. Heat the olive oil over medium-high heat and then cook the garlic, onions, and mushrooms until soft.

2. Mix with the gravy. Reserve the gravy mixture in the Roaster Pan.

3. Lay 1 Swiss cheese slice on each bread slice.

4. Top each bottom bread slice with the roast beef and then the gravy mixture.

5. Cover each bottom bread slice with a top bread slice, cheese side down.

6. Place the Grill Pan on the stove top. Butter and then grill each side of the sandwiches over medium heat until the cheese is melted and the bread is golden brown.

Eric's Tip: Oven-roasted turkey breast with cheddar cheese works just as well as the roast beef in this recipe!

Muffaletta Panini

Ingredients

Olive Salad

1 cup mixed cured olives

½ cup olive oil

1 tbsp. minced onion

1 clove garlic

1 tsp. ground black pepper

———

8 slices provolone cheese

2 ciabatta sandwich rolls, cut lengthwise

2 oz salami, sliced

3 oz ham, sliced

3 oz capicola, sliced

3 oz mortadella, sliced

¼ cup margarine, divided

Directions

1. Place the Wonder Cooker's Grill Pan on the stove top. Preheat the Grill Pan over medium heat.

2. Combine the olive salad ingredients in a food processor and then pulse to combine.

3. Place 2 provolone cheese slices on the cut side of each roll half.

4. Evenly divide the salami, ham, capicola, and mortadella between the bottom halves of the rolls.

5. Top with ½ cup olive salad and then cover with the roll's top half, cheese side down.

6. Butter and then grill each side of the sandwiches over medium heat until the cheese is melted and the bread is golden brown.

Eric's Tip: The muffaletta is one of the few sandwiches that's better the next day. The olive salad essentially marinates the sandwich and develops an amazing flavor profile.

Pastrami Coleslaw Panini

SERVES 2

Ingredients

2 tbsp. yellow mustard

4 slices pumpernickel bread

8 slices Swiss cheese

6 oz pastrami, sliced

¼ cup coleslaw

¼ cup margarine

Directions

1. Spread the mustard on one side of each bread slice.

2. Top the mustard side of each piece of bread with 2 Swiss cheese slices.

3. Divide the pastrami evenly between the bottom bread slices.

4. Top the pastrami with the coleslaw.

5. Top each bottom bread slice with a top bread slice, cheese side down.

6. Place the Wonder Cooker's Grill Pan on the stove top. Butter and then grill each side of the sandwiches over medium heat until the cheese is melted and the bread is golden brown.

Eric's Tip: You can make a "Rachel" panini by substituting turkey for the pastrami.

Braised Beef Grilled Cheese

SERVES 2

Ingredients

6 oz leftover beef brisket

½ cup BBQ sauce

8 slices cheddar cheese

4 slices whole wheat bread

4 slices pickle

¼ cup margarine

Directions

1. Combine the brisket and BBQ sauce in a bowl and mix.

2. Place 2 cheddar cheese slices on each bread slice.

3. Top the bottom bread slices with half of the beef brisket mix and then 2 pickle slices.

4. Cover each bottom bread slice with a top bread slice, cheese side down.

5. Place the Wonder Cooker's Grill Pan on the stove top. Butter and then grill each side of the sandwiches over medium heat until the cheese is melted and the bread is golden brown.

Eric's Tip: For a south-of-the-border flair on this recipe, try using pulled pork and salsa verde!

Guacamole Grilled Cheese

Ingredients

16 slices spicy pepper jack cheese

8 slices country white bread or 4 Portuguese rolls

8 tbsp. prepared guacamole

½ cup margarine

Directions

1. Layer 2 pepper jack cheese slices on each bread slice.

2. Spoon 2 tbsp. guacamole onto each bottom slice (3 tbsp. if using Portuguese rolls.)

3. Cover each bottom bread slice with a top bread slice, cheese side down.

4. Place the Wonder Cooker's Grill Pan on the stove top. Butter and then grill each side of the sandwiches over medium heat until the cheese is melted and the bread is golden brown.

Eric's Tip: Adding crispy bacon strips to this grilled cheese will take it to the next level!

Pizza Grilled Cheese

SERVES 4

Ingredients

8 slices mozzarella cheese

8 slices pepperoni

4 club rolls, cut in half

½ lb roasted red peppers

½ cup margarine

Directions

1. Place 1 mozzarella cheese slice and 1 pepperoni slice on the cut side of each roll half.

2. Layer 2 oz roasted red peppers on each roll's bottom half.

3. Cover each roll's bottom half with the roll's top half, cheese side down.

4. Place the Wonder Cooker's Grill Pan on the stove top. Butter and then grill each side of the sandwiches over medium heat until the cheese is melted and the bread is golden brown.

Eric's Tip: One delicious variation on this grilled cheese uses hot capicola, sharp provolone, and sweet bell peppers.

Monte Cristo

Ingredients

Egg Batter

2 eggs

¼ cup heavy cream

½ tsp. salt

½ tsp. cinnamon

———

5 qts. vegetable oil

8 slices Swiss cheese

4 slices white bread

¼ lb sliced turkey

¼ lb sliced ham

1 tsp. powdered sugar
(optional)

Directions

1. Whisk together the egg batter ingredients in a bowl. Reserve the egg batter in the bowl.

2. Place the Wonder Cooker's Roaster Pan on the stove top. Heat the vegetable oil over high heat until the temperature reaches 350° F/175° C.

3. Lay 1 Swiss cheese slice on each piece of bread.

4. Top each bottom bread slice with the turkey and ham.

5. Cover each bottom bread slice with a top bread slice, cheese side down.

6. Dip the sandwiches in the egg batter and then deep fry them in the Roaster Pan.

7. Dust with powdered sugar.

Eric's Tip: Don't forget the classic accoutrement of tangy red currant jelly.

Taco Sliders

Ingredients

4 lb 85% lean ground beef

1 egg

¼ cup unseasoned breadcrumbs

4 1.25-oz packages taco seasoning

24 slider rolls, cut in half

1 15.5-oz jar salsa, drained

½ cup queso blanco

3 cups shredded cheddar cheese

¼ cup diced onion

1 cup crushed tortilla chips

1 tbsp. butter, melted

Directions

1. Preheat the oven to 375° F/190° C.

2. Combine the beef, egg, breadcrumbs, and taco seasoning in a bowl to make the beef mixture.

3. Pack the beef mixture onto the Wonder Cooker's Grill Pan to form an even sheet.

4. Place the Grill Pan in the oven and bake at 375° F/190° C until the beef reaches an internal temperature of 150° F/65° C (about 30–40 mins.).

5. Remove the Grill Pan from the oven and let the beef cool slightly.

6. Place a cutting board over the top of the Grill Pan and invert the Grill Pan to transfer the beef to the cutting board.

7. Reduce the oven's temperature to 350° F/175° C.

8. Line the Roaster Pan with the rolls' bottom halves, cut side facing up, and then top with the beef.

9. Top the beef with the salsa, queso blanco, cheddar cheese, onion, and tortilla chips.

10. Cover each roll's bottom half with the top half and brush with the melted butter.

11. Cover the Roaster Pan with the Glass Lid, place the Roaster Pan in the oven, and bake at 350° F/175° C until the cheese is melted and the bread is golden brown.

Eric's Tip: I love to split the beef mixture with a spicy chorizo to add a nice kick to these sliders!

Chicken Cordon Bleu Sliders

SERVES 8–12

Ingredients

3 lb ground chicken

¼ tsp. salt

¼ tsp. ground black pepper

1 egg

½ cup breadcrumbs

24 slider rolls

¾ lb sliced ham

½ lb sliced Swiss cheese

½ cup Russian dressing

1 tbsp. butter, melted

Directions

1. Preheat the oven to 350° F/175° C

2. Combine the ground chicken, salt, ground black pepper, egg, and breadcrumbs in a large bowl and mix thoroughly.

3. Pack the chicken onto the Wonder Cooker's Grill Pan to form an even sheet.

4. Place the Grill Pan in the oven and bake at 350° F/175° C until the chicken reaches an internal temperature of 165° F/74° C (about 30–40 mins.).

5. Remove the chicken from the oven and let cool slightly.

6. Place a cutting board over the top of the Grill Pan and invert the Grill Pan to transfer the chicken to the cutting board.

7. Line the bottom of the Roaster Pan with rolls' bottom halves, cut side facing up, and top with the chicken.

8. Top the chicken with the ham, Swiss cheese, and Russian dressing.

9. Cover each roll's bottom half with the top half and brush with melted butter.

10. Cover the Roaster Pan with the Glass Lid, place in the oven, and bake at 350° F/175° C until heated through (about 20–25 mins.).

Eric's Tip: My slider roll of choice with this recipe is a potato-style roll that's similar to a sweet brioche.

Potato- & Bacon-Stuffed
Hamburgers

SERVES 4

Ingredients

24 oz ground beef

4 tbsp. pre-prepared mashed potatoes

4 bacon slices, cooked & diced

8 tbsp. shredded cheddar cheese

Directions

1. Divide the ground beef into eight 3-oz balls. Form the balls into patties.

2. Push in the center of four of the patties to make cavities. Fill each cavity with 1 tbsp. mashed potatoes, 1 diced bacon slice, and 2 tbsp. cheddar cheese.

3. Top each stuffed patty with an unstuffed patty and crimp the edges to seal.

4. Place the Wonder Cooker's Grill Pan on the stove top. Grill each side of the patties over medium-high heat until the desired doneness is reached (5–7 mins. per side).

Eric's Tip: For a different version, I'll use ground turkey, mashed sweet potato, and diced ham, then top it off with a little pineapple salsa.

Italian Sausage & Pepper Sliders

Ingredients

3 lb ground Italian sausage

2 tbsp. olive oil

2 yellow onions, sliced

1 red pepper, sliced

1 yellow pepper, sliced

1 orange pepper, sliced

1 green pepper, sliced

1 ½ cups jarred tomato sauce

3 cups shredded mozzarella cheese

Garlic Butter

2 tbsp. butter, melted

3 cloves garlic, minced

Directions

1. Preheat the oven to 350° F/175° C.

2. Pack the sausage evenly into the Wonder Cooker's Grill Pan.

3. Place the Grill Pan in the oven and bake at 350° F/175° C until the sausage reaches an internal temperature of 170° F/75° C (about 30–40 mins.).

4. While the sausage bakes, place the Roaster Pan on the stove top. Heat the olive oil over medium heat and then sauté the onion and peppers until soft (about 5–10 mins). Transfer to a bowl and set aside.

5. When the sausage is done cooking, remove from the oven and let cool slightly.

6. Place a cutting board over the top of the Grill Pan and invert the Grill Pan to transfer the sausage to the cutting board.

7. Line the Roaster Pan with rolls' bottom halves, cut side facing up, and then top with the sausage.

8. Top the sausage with the peppers, onions, tomato sauce, and mozzarella cheese.

9. Combine the butter and garlic in a bowl and microwave for 1–2 mins.

10. Cover each roll's bottom half with the top half and brush with the melted garlic butter.

11. Cover the Roaster Pan with the Glass Lid, transfer the Roaster Pan to the oven, and bake at 350° F/175° C until the cheese is melted and the bread is golden brown.

Eric's Tip: Serve these little treats with a spicy arrabbiata sauce for dipping!

POULTRY

Crunchy Baked BBQ Chicken Legs

Eric's Tarragon Brine-Infused Fried Chicken

Sesame-Crusted Chicken Tenders

Grilled Cilantro Lime Chicken with Fresh Salsa

Savory Roasted Chicken

Chicken Cordon Bleu

Chicken & White Bean Cassoulet

Sausage- & Apple-Stuffed Turkey

Chicken Cacciatore

Red Wine-Braised Turkey Leg

Coq au Vin

Parmesan-Crusted Chicken Cutlets
with Mustard Vinaigrette

Crunchy Baked BBQ Chicken Legs

SERVES 6

Ingredients

2 tsp. salt

1 tsp. ground black pepper

2 tbsp. paprika

1 tsp. garlic powder

1 tsp. onion powder

1 cup canned crispy fried onions, crushed

12 drumsticks

2 cups BBQ sauce

Directions

1. Combine the salt, ground black pepper, paprika, garlic powder, onion powder, and crispy fried onions in a bowl to make the seasoning.

2. Rub the seasoning all over the drumsticks and let sit for 30 mins.

3. Preheat the oven to 375° F/190° C.

4. Place the drumsticks in the Wonder Cooker's Roaster Pan, place the Roaster Pan in the oven, and bake at 375° F/190° C for 35 until the drumsticks reach an internal temperature of 165° F/74° C (40–45 mins.).

5. Brush with your favorite BBQ sauce.

Eric's Tip: If you use boneless chicken thighs, this dish makes a great taco filling!

Fried Chicken

SERVES 6

Ingredients

1 tsp. olive oil

1 yellow onion, sliced thinly

4 cloves garlic, chopped

7 cups water

1 cup kosher salt

½ cup sugar

6 sprigs thyme

7 sprigs tarragon

4 chicken thighs

4 chicken legs

2 chicken breasts, cut in half lengthwise

1 qt. buttermilk

3 cups flour

3 tbsp. paprika

1 tbsp. turmeric

2 tsp. ground black pepper

2 tbsp. onion powder

1 tsp. ground cayenne pepper

5 qts. canola oil

Directions

1. Place the Wonder Cooker's Roaster Pan on the stove top. Heat the olive oil over medium heat, add the onion and garlic, and sauté for 3 mins.

2. Add the water, salt, sugar, thyme, and tarragon and bring to boil to make the brine. Lower the heat to low and simmer for 5 mins. Then, let the brine cool.

3. Once cooled, add the chicken thighs, legs, and breasts; cover the Roaster Pan with the Grill Pan; and refrigerate overnight.

4. Preheat the oven to 350° F/175° C.

5. Pour the buttermilk into a bowl.

6. Combine the flour, paprika, turmeric, ground black pepper, onion powder, and ground cayenne pepper in a baking dish to make the flour mixture.

7. Remove the chicken from the brine and remove the brine from the Roaster Pan.

8. Place the Roaster Pan on the stove top. Heat the canola oil over medium-high heat until the temperature reaches 325° F/160° C.

9. Dip the chicken pieces in the buttermilk and then the flour mixture.

10. Fry the chicken in the Roaster Pan until golden brown (10–15 mins.).

11. Carefully move the chicken from the Roaster Pan to the Grill Pan. Place the Grill Pan in the oven and cook at 350° F/175° C until the internal temperature of the chicken reaches 165° F/75° C.

Eric's Tip: This brine recipe works just as well with bone-in pork chops. This method is great for lean cuts of meat.

Sesame-Crusted Chicken Tenders

SERVES 6

Ingredients

½ cup soy sauce

½ cup water

2 tbsp. extra virgin oil

2 tbsp. lemon juice

1 tbsp. brown sugar

1 large clove garlic, grated

½-in. piece of ginger, peeled & grated

2 lb chicken tenders

3 tbsp. canola oil

4 egg whites, beaten with a fork

1 cup cornstarch

1 ½ cups sesame seeds

1 cup chopped scallions

Directions

1. Combine the soy sauce, water, olive oil, lemon juice, brown sugar, garlic, and ginger in a glass bowl.

2. Add the chicken tenders and marinate for 1 hr. in the refrigerator.

3. Place the Wonder Cooker's Roaster Pan on the stove top. Heat the canola oil over medium heat.

4. Whisk the egg whites in a glass baking dish.

5. Add the cornstarch to a second baking dish.

6. Pour the sesame seeds into a third baking dish.

7. Dip the marinated chicken tenders in the cornstarch and then the egg whites. Finally, coat the chicken in the sesame seeds.

8. Sauté the chicken in the Grill Pan until golden brown (about 5 mins. per side).

9. Top the chicken with the scallions when serving.

Eric's Tip: This recipe is a great way to introduce shrimp and scallops to picky eaters. Just substitute the shrimp or scallops for the chicken tenders and follow the same instructions.

Grilled Cilantro Lime Chicken

with Fresh Salsa

Ingredients

2 tbsp. olive oil

zest of 2 limes

¼ cup fresh lime juice

1 tsp. cumin

½ tsp. sugar

½ tsp. salt

¼ tsp. ground black pepper

3 cloves garlic, minced

½ cup chopped cilantro

2 lb boneless chicken breasts, pounded

Salsa

1 pint tri-color cherry tomatoes, halved

¼ red onion, diced

½ jalapeño pepper, sliced thinly

1 tsp. lime zest

2 tsp. lime juice

¼ tsp. salt

1 tsp. crushed red pepper flakes

1 avocado, peeled & diced

Directions

1. Combine the olive oil, lime juice and zest, cumin, sugar, salt, ground black pepper, garlic, and cilantro in a glass baking dish. Add the chicken breasts and marinate for 30 mins.

2. Place the Wonder Cooker's Grill Pan on the stove top. Preheat the Grill Pan over medium-high heat and then grill each side of the chicken breasts for 5 mins.

3. Combine the salsa ingredients in a bowl. Serve the salsa on top of the chicken breasts.

Eric's Tip: If you substitute skirt steak for the chicken, you'll get a delicious carne asada-style dish.

Savory Roasted Chicken

SERVES 8

Ingredients

Seasonings

1 tsp. kosher salt

1 tsp. ground black pepper

1 tsp. turmeric

1 tsp. onion powder

1 tsp. garlic powder

1 tbsp. thyme

1 tbsp. basil

1 tsp. marjoram

1 tbsp. dried rosemary

———

2 4-lb chickens

4 tbsp. melted butter

1 lemon, halved & juiced

6 rosemary sprigs

Directions

1. Preheat the oven to 350° F/175° C.

2. Combine the seasonings in a bowl and mix.

3. Remove the giblets from the cavities of the chickens.

4. Rub the chickens with the butter and lemon juice and then sprinkle the seasonings on the chicken.

5. Take the juiced lemon halves and place one in each chicken's cavity along with the rosemary sprigs.

6. Place the chickens in the Wonder Cooker's Roaster Pan. Place the Roaster Pan in the oven and bake at 350° F/175° C until the internal temperature of the chicken reaches 165° F/74° C (1 1/2–2 hrs.).

Eric's Tip: This classic chicken needs to be served with roasted fingerling potatoes tossed in garlic, butter, and parsley.

Chicken Cordon Bleu

SERVES 8

Ingredients

8 boneless chicken breasts, cut thinly

2 tsp. salt

1 tsp. ground black pepper

8 slices prosciutto

8 slices Gruyère cheese

1 cup flour

4 eggs, beaten

2 cups breadcrumbs

¼ cup olive oil

Directions

1. Preheat the oven to 375° F/190° C.

2. Pound the chicken breasts thin and then season with the salt and ground black pepper. Place the prosciutto and Gruyère cheese in the center of each cutlet and then roll and secure with toothpicks.

3. Pour the flour into a pan.

4. Add the beaten eggs to a second pan.

5. Place the breadcrumbs in a third pan.

6. Dip each stuffed breast into the flour, then the egg, and finally the breadcrumbs.

7. Place the Wonder Cooker's Grill Pan on the stove top. Lightly coat the bottom of the Grill Pan with the olive oil. Heat the olive oil over medium heat.

8. Fry the chicken rolls until golden all over.

9. Place the Grill Pan in the oven and bake at 375° F/190° C until the internal temperature of the chicken reaches 165° F/75° C (20–25 mins.).

Eric's Tip: Serve these crispy delights over some sautéed garlicky greens!

Chicken & White Bean Cassoulet

Ingredients

2 tbsp. olive oil

1 lb chicken legs

1 lb chicken thighs

1 tbsp. salt

2 tsp. ground black pepper, divided

2 links Italian sausage, sliced

2 garlic cloves, minced

2 leeks, washed & chopped

4 carrots, sliced

3 cups chicken broth

¼ cup white vermouth

2 cups water

1 tsp. kosher salt

¼ tsp. ground black pepper

1 lb white beans, soaked overnight, drained & rinsed

2 bay leaves

4 sprigs thyme

2 sprigs parsley

Directions

1. Preheat the oven to 350° F/175° C.

2. Season the chicken legs and thighs with with the salt and 1 ½ tsp. ground black pepper.

3. Place the Wonder Cooker's Roaster Pan on the stove top. Heat the olive oil over medium-high heat and then sear the chicken legs and thighs until brown (about 8 mins.).

4. Remove the chicken and add the sausage.

5. Cook the sausage for 8 mins. Remove and reserve the sausage.

6. Add the garlic, leeks, carrots, chicken broth, vermouth, water, salt, ground black pepper, beans, bay leaves, thyme, and parsley. Bring to a boil and add the chicken and sausage.

7. Cover the Roaster Pan with the Grill Pan, transfer to the oven, and cook at 350° F/175° C for 1 ½ hrs.

Eric's Tip: Traditionally, this dish uses a mix of sausages, so pick up a variety at your local market!

Sausage- & Apple-Stuffed Turkey

SERVES 12

Ingredients

1 tbsp. olive oil

4 links Italian sausage, chopped

2 cloves garlic, chopped

1 cup sliced leeks

2 tbsp. thyme

¼ cup fresh sage

4 oz shiitake mushroom caps, sliced

2 large portobello mushrooms, chopped

2 green apples, diced

½ cup white wine

1–1 ½ cups chicken stock*

3 ½ cups wild blend rice, cooked

3 cups stuffing cubes

1 16-lb turkey

1 cup chicken broth

Directions

1. Preheat the oven to 350° F/175° C.

2. Place the Wonder Cooker's Roaster Pan on the stove top. Heat the olive oil over medium heat and then cook the sausage for 6–8 mins.

3. Add the garlic, leeks, thyme, and sage to the Roaster Pan and cook for 3 mins.

4. Add the shiitake and portobello mushrooms and the apples to the Roaster Pan and cook for 1 min.

5. Add the wine and stock. Bring the wine and stock to a boil over high heat. Remove the Roaster Pan from the heat and add the rice and stuffing cubes.

6. Loosely stuff the turkey and place it in the Roaster Pan. Add the chicken broth to the Roaster Pan.

7. Transfer the Roaster Pan to the oven and roast at 350° F/175° C until the turkey reaches an internal temperature of 165° F/74° C (3–3 1/2 hrs.), basting every 20 mins. while roasting.

*The amount of stock used in this recipe varies depending on the density and desired moisture of the stuffing.

Eric's Tip: I love taking the leftovers the next day and making a Thanksgiving sandwich. Don't forget the cranberry sauce!

Chicken Cacciatore

Ingredients

12 chicken thighs

2 tsp. salt

1 tsp. ground black pepper

¼ cup olive oil

1 yellow onion, sliced

1 green bell pepper, sliced

1 red bell pepper, sliced

1 lb button mushrooms, sliced

2 cloves garlic, minced

1 cup red wine

½ cup dry vermouth

2 tbsp. tomato paste

2 14-oz cans fire-roasted tomatoes

1 tbsp. oregano

1 ½ cups tomato sauce

10 basil leaves

Directions

1. Preheat the oven to 350° F/175° C.

2. Season the chicken thighs with the salt and ground black pepper.

3. Place the Wonder Cooker's Roaster Pan on the stove top. Heat the olive oil over medium-high heat. Brown both sides of the chicken. Remove from the Roaster Pan.

4. Sauté the onion and green and red bell pepper in the Roaster Pan for 5 mins.

5. Add the mushrooms, garlic, wine, vermouth, tomato paste, tomatoes, oregano, tomato sauce, and basil.

6. Return the chicken to the Roaster Pan, transfer to the oven, and cook at 350° F/175° C for 1 ½ hrs.

Eric's Tip: This dish deserves nothing less than to be served over fresh fettuccini. The rich sauce will get soaked up by the pasta.

Red Wine-Braised Turkey Leg

Ingredients

2 tsp. salt

1 tsp. ground black pepper

1 tbsp. oregano

1 cup flour, divided

6 turkey legs

⅓ cup canola oil

2 large leeks, chopped

4 stalks celery, chopped

8 small carrots, tops & greens trimmed, halved lengthwise

4 cloves garlic, minced

4 cups dry red wine

2 qts. chicken stock

5 sprigs thyme

2 bay leaves

Directions

1. Preheat the oven to 350° F/175° C.

2. Combine the salt, ground black pepper, oregano, and ½ cup flour in a bowl to make the flour mixture.

3. Dust the turkey legs with the flour mixture.

4. Place the Wonder Cooker's Roaster Pan on the stove top. Heat the canola oil over medium heat. Add the turkey legs and brown all sides. Remove and reserve the turkey legs.

5. Add the leeks, celery, carrots, and garlic to the Roaster Pan and cook for 5 mins.

6. Add the wine and chicken stock to the Roaster Pan and then add the thyme and bay leaves.

7. Return the turkey legs to the Roaster Pan, cover with the Glass Lid, transfer to the oven, and bake at 350° F/175° C for 2–2 ½ hrs.

8. Remove the turkey legs and place on a serving platter.

9. Stir ½ cup flour and some broth from the Roaster Pan together in a bowl. Pour the new flour mixture back into the Roaster Pan and cook over high heat until the mixture is reduced by half and a thick sauce is formed.

10. Serve the turkey legs with the sauce.

Eric's Tip: After cooking, I'll hand shred the turkey and mix it with the vegetables to make pulled turkey sliders.

Coq au Vin

Ingredients

2 tsp. salt

1 tsp. ground black pepper

1 ¼ cups flour, divided

6 chicken legs

6 chicken thighs

2 chicken breasts, split in half

¼ cup olive oil

6 strips bacon, chopped

1 lb carrots, cut diagonally

1 14.4-oz bag frozen pearl onions

1 lb button mushrooms, quartered

3 cloves garlic, minced

½ cup brandy

3 cups red wine

8 sprigs thyme

1 bay leaf

1 ½ cups chicken broth

4 tbsp. butter, softened

½ cup chopped Italian parsley

Directions

1. Preheat the oven to 350° F/175° C.

2. Combine the salt, ground black pepper, and 1 cup flour in a bowl.

3. Dredge the chicken legs, thighs, and breasts in the flour.

4. Place the Wonder Cooker's Roaster Pan on the stove top. Heat the olive oil over medium-high heat and then sear the chicken until brown (about 10 mins.). Remove and set aside.

5. Add the bacon to the Roaster Pan and sauté until crisp. Remove and set aside.

6. Add the carrots, onions, mushrooms, and garlic to the Roaster Pan and sauté for 5 mins.

7. Remove the Roaster Pan from the heat and add the brandy. Return the Roaster Pan to the stove top and reduce the brandy by half. Add the wine and cook for 5 mins.

8. Add the thyme, bay leaf, chicken broth, and chicken to the Roaster Pan and bring to boil.

9. Transfer the Roaster Pan to the oven and cook at 350° F/175° C for 45 mins.

10. Remove the Roaster Pan from the oven. Combine the butter and ¼ cup flour in a bowl and then stir into the sauce to thicken. Stir in the parsley and bacon before serving.

Eric's Tip: This recipe is so complex with flavor that it's always better the next day. Don't be afraid to make it the day before and let it cool overnight.

Parmesan-Crusted Chicken Cutlets
with Mustard Vinaigrette

Ingredients

2 tbsp. olive oil

1 cup flour

4 eggs, beaten

1 cup shredded Parmesan cheese

¾ cup grated Parmesan cheese

6 boneless chicken breasts, pounded 1/4-in. thick

Mustard Vinaigrette

1 clove garlic, minced

3 tbsp. Champagne vinegar

1 tbsp. Dijon mustard

1 tsp. honey

½ tsp. salt

¼ tsp. ground black pepper

¾ cup olive oil

mixed greens, for serving

Directions

1. Place the Wonder Cooker's Roaster Pan on the stove top. Heat 2 tbsp. olive oil over medium heat.

2. Pour the flour into a bowl.

3. Beat the eggs in a second bowl.

4. Combine the shredded and grated Parmesan cheese in a third bowl.

5. Dip the chicken breasts in the flour, then the egg, and finally the cheese.

6. Fry the chicken in the Roaster Pan (5 mins. per side).

7. Whisk together the garlic, vinegar, mustard, honey, salt, and ground black pepper in a small bowl. Slowly whisk in ¾ cup olive oil to finish the mustard vinaigrette.

8. Serve the chicken with the mustard vinaigrette and mixed greens.

Eric's Tip: For a different spin on this dish, grab fresh red snapper fillets from your local fish market to use instead of chicken.

SOUPS & STEWS

French Onion Soup

Bacon Cheeseburger Soup

Cajun Jambalaya

Veal & Pepper Stew

Irish Lamb Stew

White Chicken Chili

Pork & Bean Ragout

Manhattan Clam Chowder

Louisiana Gumbo

Portuguese Clam Stew with Chorizo

Zuppa de Pesce

Thai Coconut Bouillabaisse

French Onion Soup

Ingredients

10 onions, sliced

1 stick butter

2 bay leaves

5 sprigs thyme

10 cups brown stock

¾ cup brandy

16 slices of French bread, toasted

24 slices Gruyère cheese

Directions

1. Place the Wonder Cooker's Roaster Pan on the stove top. Sweat the onions in the butter over medium-low heat until the onions are caramelized.

2. Add the bay leaves, thyme, brown stock, and brandy.

3. Let simmer for about 40 mins.

4. Turn the broiler on high.

5. Ladle the soup into onion soup crocks and top with the French bread and Gruyère cheese.

6. Transfer the Roaster Pan to the broiler and bake until the cheese is melted and golden brown.

Eric's Tip: I love to add another layer of flavor by making toasted garlic bread to melt under the cheese!

Bacon Cheeseburger Soup

Ingredients

3 sticks butter, divided

1 onion, sliced

1 lb carrots, sliced

3 stalks celery, chopped

1 red pepper, chopped

4 cups baby potatoes, quartered

2 ½ lb ground beef

6 cups chicken broth

2 tsp. salt

½ tsp. ground black pepper

1 tsp. Worcestershire sauce

3 cups milk

¾ cups flour

2 lb non-dairy cheese, cubed

10 strips bacon, cooked

Directions

1. Place the Wonder Cooker's Roaster Pan on the stove top. Preheat over medium heat, cook the beef, drain, and set aside.

2. Melt 2 sticks of the butter and then add the onion, carrots, celery, and red pepper. Cook for 5 mins.

3. Add the potatoes, beef, and chicken broth and bring to a boil.

4. Add the salt, ground black pepper, and Worcestershire sauce. Simmer for 10 mins. and then add the milk.

5. Melt 1 stick of butter in a bowl. Add the flour, mix until smooth, and then add to the Roaster Pan.

6. Add the non-dairy cheese, stirring until it melts.

7. Cook the soup until the potatoes are tender (about 45 mins.).

8. Top with the bacon and serve.

Eric's Tip: I love to put a fiesta flair on this recipe by adding chopped chipotle peppers and topping with crispy tortilla strips, pico de gallo, and fresh cilantro.

Cajun Jambalaya

SERVES 12

Ingredients

¼ cup canola oil

3 cups diced onion

1 cup diced celery

6 cloves garlic, minced

1 cup diced green bell pepper

1 ½ lb Andouille sausage, sliced

2 ½ lb chicken, white and dark meat cut into 1-in. cubes

2 tbsp. tomato paste

3 cups long-grain rice

2 cups water

4 cups chicken stock

2 tbsp. salt

3 bay leaves

½ tsp. ground cayenne pepper

1 cup chopped scallion greens

Directions

1. Place the Wonder Cooker's Roaster Pan on the stove top. Heat the canola oil over medium heat and then sauté the onion, celery, garlic, and green bell pepper for 8 mins.

2. Add the sausage and cook for 7–10 mins.

3. Add the chicken and cook for 5–7 mins.

4. Add the tomato paste and cook for 3 mins.

5. Add the rice, stir, and then cook for 2 mins.

6. Add the water, chicken stock, salt, bay leaves, and ground cayenne pepper. Cover with the Grill Pan and cook over medium heat for 20 mins. without removing the Grill Pan or stirring.

7. Turn off the heat and let rest for 10 mins.

8. Remove the Grill Pan, mix in the scallion greens, remove the bay leaves, and serve.

Eric's Tip: Sometimes, I'll skip the rice and serve it over fresh fettucine tossed with butter and Cajun seasoning for a N'awlins-style pasta.

Veal & Pepper Stew

Ingredients

4 lb veal, cubed

½ cup flour

3 tbsp. olive oil

2 cups red wine

3 garlic cloves, chopped

1 tsp. salt

½ tsp. ground black pepper

½ cup chopped fresh sage

2 14 ½-oz cans diced tomatoes

2 cups chicken broth

1 onion, sliced

2 red bell peppers, sliced

2 green bell peppers, sliced

Directions

1. Coat the veal with the flour.

2. Place the Wonder Cooker's Roaster Pan on the stove top. Heat the olive oil over medium heat and sauté the veal in batches until brown. Remove and set aside.

3. Add the wine and scrape the residue at the bottom of the Roaster Pan. Add the garlic, bring to a boil, and reduce by half.

4. Add the salt, ground black pepper, sage, tomatoes, and chicken broth and then cook for 3 mins.

5. Return the veal to the pan; add the onion, red bell peppers, and green bell peppers; cover with the Grill Pan; and simmer for 1 ½ hrs.

Eric's Tip: If veal is not available, you can use cubed pork shoulder with similar results. I've also used skinless chicken thighs in this recipe as well.

Irish Lamb Stew

Ingredients

3 ½ lb lamb meat

½ cup flour

¼ cup olive oil

3 tbsp. butter

3 cloves garlic, minced

1 onion, diced

1 12-oz stout beer

2 cups brown stock

1 tsp. sea salt

1 tsp. ground black pepper

2 tbsp. tomato paste

4 celery stalks, sliced large

4 sprigs tarragon

12 baby carrots

1 bay leaf

10 baby potatoes

Directions

1. Place the lamb meat in a bowl and dust with the flour.

2. Place the Wonder Cooker's Roaster Pan on the stove top. Heat the olive oil over high heat and then brown the lamb meat.

3. Preheat the oven to 375° F/190° C.

4. Add the butter, garlic, and onion and cook for 3–4 mins.

5. Pour in the beer and brown stock and stir.

6. Add the salt, ground black pepper, tomato paste, celery, tarragon, carrots, bay leaf, and potatoes and bring to a boil.

7. Cover with the Grill Pan, place in the oven, and cook at 375° F/190° C until the meat is tender (about 2 hrs.).

Eric's Tip: I always pair this Irish stew with boiled cabbage scented with caraway seed to complement the fresh tarragon.

White Chicken Chili

SERVES 12

Ingredients

2 tbsp. olive oil

2 lb boneless chicken breast, cubed

1 large onion, chopped

3 cloves garlic, chopped

2 qts. chicken stock

2 tbsp. chopped green chilis

kernels of 2 ears corn, roasted

2 tsp. cumin

½ tsp. ground cayenne pepper

½ cup chopped cilantro

3 14 ½-oz cans white kidney beans

Directions

1. Place the Wonder Cooker's Roaster Pan on the stove top. Heat the olive oil over medium heat and then cook the chicken until light brown.

2. Add the onion, garlic, chicken stock, green chilis, corn kernels, cumin, ground cayenne pepper, cilantro, and kidney beans and simmer for 35 mins.

Eric's Tip: This recipe can be very easily changed to a vegetarian or vegan style. I'll use tempeh, seitan, or soy chorizo instead of the chicken and then add vegetable stock.

Pork & Bean Ragout

SERVES 12

Ingredients

¼ cup olive oil

5 lb boneless pork shoulder, fat removed & meat cut into 1–2-in. cubes

3 lb chorizo, cubed

3 medium onions, diced

6 carrots, diced

6 celery stalks, diced

12 oz shiitake mushrooms, sliced

12 cloves garlic, minced

6 oz tomato paste

3 15-oz cans fire-roasted tomatoes, diced

6 cups beef stock

2 tbsp. Italian seasoning

¼ tsp. salt

¼ tsp. ground black pepper

1 lb dry white beans, soaked overnight

zest of 1 lemon

Directions

1. Preheat the oven to 375° F/190° C.

2. Place the Wonder Cooker's Roaster Pan on the stove top. Heat the olive oil over medium-high heat and brown the pork in batches. Remove and reserve the pork.

3. Brown the chorizo. Remove and reserve the chorizo.

4. Sauté the onions, carrots, and celery until soft (about 6 mins.).

5. Add the mushrooms and garlic and cook for 2 mins.

6. Add the tomato paste and cook for 1 min.

7. Add the tomatoes, beef stock, Italian seasoning, salt, and ground black pepper and then simmer for 15 mins.

8. Add the pork, sausage, and beans; bring to boil; and cover with the Grill Pan.

9. Transfer the Roaster Pan to the oven and bake at 375° F/190° C for 2 hrs.

10. Remove from the oven, add the lemon zest, and mix.

Eric's Tip: To give this ragout a richer flavor, bake in the oven uncovered then stir occasionally as the top browns. This will deepen the color and intensify the flavor. You can also use different sausages to fit your tastes.

Manhattan Clam Chowder

SERVES 8

Ingredients

½ lb bacon, diced

2 onions, diced

2 carrots, diced

1 shallot, minced

½ green pepper, diced

4 celery stalks, diced small

6 6 ½-oz cans chopped clams

1 cup clam broth

4 red potatoes, diced

1 bay leaf

1 28-oz can tomatoes in juice

4 sprigs thyme

¼ cup chopped parsley

½ tsp. salt

½ tsp. ground black pepper

Directions

1. Place the Wonder Cooker's Roaster Pan on the stove top. Cook the bacon over medium-high heat until brown.

2. Add the onions, carrots, shallot, green pepper, and celery and sauté for 4 mins.

3. Strain the clams and add the juice to the Roaster Pan. Set the clams aside.

4. Add the clam broth, potatoes, bay leaf, tomatoes, and thyme.

5. Simmer for 40 mins.

6. Turn off the heat and add the clams, parsley, salt, and ground black pepper.

Eric's Tip: You can easily turn this into a cioppino-style stew by adding a variety of fresh fish and seafood like mussels, scallops, red snapper, and king crab legs. Don't forget the grilled bread!

Louisiana Gumbo

Ingredients

8 oz vegetable oil

8 oz flour

3 cups diced onion

1 ½ cups diced celery

1 ½ cups diced red bell pepper

1 ½ lb smoked cooked ham

6 tbsp. minced garlic

¾ tsp. ground cayenne pepper

1 tbsp. thyme

3 cups chicken stock

3 cups water

1 ½ tomatoes, diced

6 bay leaves

3 lb 21–25 shrimp

1 cup chopped green onion tops

½ cup chopped parsley

3 tbsp. filé powder

12 cups cooked white rice

Directions

1. Place the Wonder Cooker's Roaster Pan on the stove top. Combine the vegetable oil and flour and cook over medium heat, stirring constantly until the mixture turns the color of peanut butter.

2. Add the onion, celery, and red bell pepper and cook until soft.

3. Add the ham, garlic, ground cayenne pepper, and thyme.

4. Add the chicken stock, water, tomato, and bay leaves and whisk to combine.

5. Raise the heat to bring to a boil and reduce.

6. Lower the heat to simmer for 30 mins.

7. Add the shrimp and cook for 10 mins.

8. Add the green onion tops, parsley, and filé powder.

9. Serve in deep bowls over steamed white rice.

Eric's Tip: I love to take the leftovers and top with mashed potatoes spiked with Maryland crab seasoning to make a spicy shepherd's pie.

Portuguese Clam Stew with Chorizo

SERVES 6

Ingredients

2 tbsp. olive oil

¼ lb bacon, sliced into ½-in. pieces

½ lb cooked chorizo, sliced into-½ in. pieces

1 yellow onion, sliced thinly

1 red bell pepper, cut into thin strips

3 cloves garlic, minced

1 14-oz can fire-roasted tomatoes

1 ½ cups chicken stock

1 tsp. smoked paprika

1 bay leaf

48 littleneck clams, washed

2 cups chopped kale

2 tbsp. chopped parsley

Directions

1. Place the Wonder Cooker's Roaster Pan on the stove top. Heat the olive oil over medium heat, add the bacon and chorizo, and cook for 7 mins. Remove and reserve the bacon and chorizo.

2. Add the onions, peppers, and garlic and cook for 5 mins.

3. Add the chorizo, bacon, tomatoes, and stock and then raise the heat to bring to a boil.

4. Add the paprika and bay leaf.

5. Add the clams and kale, cover with the Grill Pan, and cook until the clams open (about 10 mins.).

6. Add the parsley before serving.

Eric's Tip: Other traditional variations on this homestyle fisherman stew include octopus and salt cod. Pouring it over roasted Yukon gold potatoes takes it to another level!

Zuppa de Pesce

SERVES 6

Ingredients

¼ cup olive oil

2 leeks, sliced

6 cloves garlic, sliced thinly

18 mussels, cleaned

1 lb flounder, cut into chunks

12 large shrimp, peeled & deveined

6 4-oz lobster tails, cut in half

1 ½ cups white wine

¼ cup lemon juice

1 lb calamari, cut into rings

1 tsp. salt

½ tsp. ground black pepper

1 tsp. red pepper flakes

5 sprigs thyme

6 cups hearty tomato sauce

18 large scallops

2 cans white kidney beans

¼ cup chopped parsley

zest of 1 lemon

Directions

1. Place the Wonder Cooker's Roaster Pan on the stove top. Heat the olive oil over medium heat and then sauté the leeks and garlic.

2. Add the rest of the ingredients and simmer until the fish is cooked and the mussels open.

Eric's Tip: The key to this dish is buying the freshest product available. You can make any combination of fish, seafood, and shellfish. I love to finish with a good spoonful of pesto sauce.

Thai Coconut Bouillabaisse

SERVES 6

Ingredients

1 tbsp. canola oil

1 lb jumbo shrimp, peeled & deveined, shells reserved

4 stalks celery, chopped, divided

3 cups carrots, cut diagonally, divided

1 leek, sliced

1 large onion, sliced, divided

2 ½ cups water

4 cloves garlic, divided

1 bay leaf

1 tsp. olive oil

2 red bell peppers, cut into 1-in. pieces

10 shiitake mushrooms, sliced

1 tsp. red curry paste

2 tbsp. grated ginger

1 13 ½-oz can coconut milk

½ cup white wine

2 tomatoes, chopped

½ lb scallops, cleaned

12 littleneck clams, washed

zest of ½ lime

½ cup fresh Thai basil

¼ cup fresh cilantro

Directions

1. Place the Wonder Cooker's Roaster Pan on the stove top. Heat the canola oil over medium-high heat, add the shrimp shells, and cook for 3 mins.

2. Add 2 chopped celery stalks, ½ cup carrots, and ½ onion and then cook for 1 min.

3. Stir in the water, 2 garlic cloves, and the bay leaf and then bring to a boil. Reduce the heat to a simmer for 30 mins. and then strain the broth through a sieve over a bowl and discard the solids.

4. Heat the olive oil over medium heat; add the remaining celery, carrots, leek, and garlic; and then cook for 3 mins.

5. Add the red bell peppers and mushrooms and then cook 1 min.

6. Stir in the curry paste, ginger, coconut milk, broth from the shrimp shells, wine, and tomatoes and bring to a boil.

7. Add the shrimp, scallops, and clams; cover with the Grill Pan; and cook until the clams open and the shrimp is cooked (5 mins.).

8. Stir in the lime zest, basil, and cilantro.

Eric's Tip: I love to pair any dish that has coconut curry with ginger and mint-scented jasmine rice. Topping it off with chopped cashews adds an exotic crunch and toasty flavor.

VEGGIES & POTATOES

Campfire Potatoes

SERVES 8–10

Ingredients

1 lb thick bacon, cut into 1-in. strips

2 onions, sliced thinly

5 lb Yukon gold potatoes, cut into ¼-in. pieces

4 cups shredded cheddar cheese

1 tbsp. salt

1 tbsp. ground black pepper

1 tbsp. garlic powder

1 12-oz bottle lager beer

6 tbsp. sour cream

1 cup chopped chives

Directions

1. Preheat the oven to 375° F/190° C.

2. Place the Wonder Cooker's Roaster Pan on the stove top. Cook the bacon in the Roaster Pan over medium heat until crisp. Remove and reserve the bacon.

3. Cook the onions in the Roaster Pan over medium heat until soft (3–5 mins.). Remove and reserve the onions.

4. Remove the Roaster Pan from the heat. Layer one quarter of the potatoes in the Roaster Pan followed by one quarter of the cheddar cheese, onion, bacon, salt, ground black pepper, and garlic powder.

5. Repeat the layering process three times.

6. Pour the beer over the casserole.

7. Cover the Roaster Pan with its Glass Lid, transfer to the oven, and bake at 375° F/190° C until tender (about 2 hrs.).

8. Top with the sour cream and chives.

Eric's Tip: These filling potatoes can stand up to a delicious smoked brisket or grilled steak to complete your meal.

Garlic Twice-Baked Potatoes

SERVES 12

Ingredients

Roasted Garlic

2 heads garlic

1 tbsp. olive oil

1 tbsp. salt

1 tsp. ground white pepper

———

10 large red potatoes

2 tbsp. butter

½ cup heavy cream

½ tsp. salt

½ tsp. ground black pepper

2 tbsp. chives

1 tbsp. onion powder

½ cup shredded cheddar cheese

¼ cup cooked & chopped bacon

Directions

1. Preheat the oven to 375° F/190° C

2. Cut the garlic heads in half, placed the cut garlic heads on foil, drizzle the olive oil over the garlic, and sprinkle the salt and ground white pepper on the garlic.

3. Wrap the garlic in foil and roast in the oven at 375° F/190° C for 1 hr.

4. Squeeze the roasted garlic cloves into a bowl and set them aside.

5. Place the potatoes in the oven and roast at 375° F/190° C until a fork can easily pierce them (about 30–45 mins.).

6. Cut the potatoes in half and scoop out the middle of each half, leaving a ¼-in. layer of potato on the inside of the skin. Reserve the scooped-out potato in a bowl.

7. Mash the reserved potato pieces together with the roasted garlic, butter, heavy cream, salt, and ground black pepper. The mixture should be lumpy.

8. Place the potato skins in the Wonder Roaster's Grill Pan and fill them with the mashed potato mix.

9. Top with the chives, onion powder, cheddar cheese, and bacon.

10. Place the Grill Pan in the oven and bake at 375° F/190° C until browned (about 20 mins.).

Eric's Tip: I love to add leftover rotisserie chicken and a touch of buffalo sauce for a game day appetizer.

Corn Spoonbread

SERVES 12

Ingredients

4 cups milk

4 cups water

2 tsp. salt

½ tsp. ground black pepper

2 tbsp. butter

2 ½ cups cornmeal

6 eggs

2 cups buttermilk

1 onion

3 cups fresh corn

1 poblano pepper, diced

1 jalapeño, diced

4 cups shredded cheddar cheese

1 tsp. onion powder

Directions

1. Place the Wonder Cooker's Roaster Pan on the stove top. Add the milk, water, salt, ground black pepper, and butter to the Roaster Pan.

2. Bring to a boil over high heat and then whisk in the cornmeal. Cook for 2 mins.

3. Separate the egg yolks from the egg whites.

4. Let the cornmeal cool for 5 mins.

5. Preheat the oven to 350° F/175° C.

6. Stir the onion, corn, poblano pepper, jalapeño, cheddar cheese, and onion powder into the Roaster Pan.

7. Fold in the egg yolks and the buttermilk.

8. Whip the whites to stiff peaks. Fold them into the cornmeal mixture.

9. Cover the Roaster Pan with the Grill Pan, transfer to the oven, and cook at 350° F/175° C for 1 hr.

10. Remove the Grill Pan and cook at 350° F/175° C for an additional 15 mins.

Eric's Tip: I love to pour a big scoop of chili over this spoonbread. Don't forget the sour cream and chives!

Sweet Potato Gratin

Ingredients

3 cups heavy cream

2 tbsp. minced garlic

4 tbsp. minced shallots

8 sprigs thyme, chopped

1 tsp. grated nutmeg

1 tsp. salt

½ tsp. ground white pepper

4 lb sweet potatoes, peeled & sliced into ⅛-in. pieces

1 cup Gruyère cheese

1 cup cheddar cheese

Directions

1. Preheat the oven to 375° F/190° C.

2. Place a saucepan on the stove top. Heat the heavy cream, garlic, shallots, thyme, nutmeg, salt, and ground black pepper in the saucepan over medium-high heat to make the cream mixture. Bring to a boil.

3. Line the bottom of the Wonder Cooker's Roaster Pan with one third of the potatoes in a single layer and sprinkle with one third of the Gruyère and cheddar cheese.

4. Repeat the layering process twice and then pour the cream mixture over the potatoes.

5. Transfer the Roaster Pan to the oven and bake at 375° F/190° C for 40 mins.

Eric's Tip: Most people think of potato gratin as a side dish at dinner. I love to serve these at brunch with poached eggs on top.

O'Brien Potatoes

SERVES 10–12

Ingredients

1 ½ tbsp. butter, divided

1 ½ tbsp. olive oil, divided

1 onion, chopped

1 red bell pepper, diced

1 green bell pepper, diced

1 tsp. salt

1 tsp. ground black pepper

¼ tsp. ground cayenne pepper

½ tsp. Worcestershire sauce

2 lb white potatoes

parsley, chopped, for garnish

Directions

1. Place the Roaster Pan on the stove top. Melt ¾ tbsp. butter in the Roaster Pan over medium heat, add ¾ tbsp. olive oil, and sauté the onion for 7 mins.

2. Add the red and green pepper, salt, ground black pepper, ground cayenne pepper, and Worcestershire sauce and continue cooking for 3–5 mins.

3. Add the potatoes, ¾ tbsp. butter, and ¾ tbsp. olive oil.

4. Cook over medium-high heat until medium brown (about 35–40 mins.).

5. Garnish with the chopped parsley.

Eric's Tip: If you have any left over, turn it into a hearty quiche filling the next day. Just add bacon!

Hard Cider-Braised Red Cabbage with Apple

SERVES 8–10

Ingredients

½ lb bacon, diced

1 large onion, sliced

2 heads red cabbage, cored & cut into thick strips

2 apples, peeled & diced large

1 cup red wine vinegar

1 12-oz bottle hard cider

¼ cup brown sugar

2 tsp. salt

¼ tsp. ground black pepper

½ tsp. allspice

Directions

1. Place the Wonder Cooker's Roaster Pan on the stove top. Sauté the bacon in the Roaster Pan over medium-high heat until golden.

2. Add the onion and sauté for 3–4 mins.

3. Lower the heat to low. Add the cabbage, apples, red wine, hard cider, brown sugar, salt, ground black pepper, and allspice.

4. Cover the Roaster Pan with the Glass Lid and simmer until tender (about 25–30 mins.).

Eric's Tip: You'll want to serve this cabbage with a tangy sauerbraten or pork schnitzel.

Roasted Root Vegetables

Ingredients

1 large butternut squash, cubed

3 Yukon potatoes, cut into 1-in. pieces

1 bunch of beets, cut into 1-in. pieces

1 red onion, cut into 1-in. pieces

2 parsnips, cut into 1-in. pieces

1 head of garlic, peeled & cloves separated

2 tbsp. olive oil

1 ½ tsp. salt

1 tsp. ground black pepper

1 tbsp. chopped rosemary

1 tbsp. chopped sage

½ cup toasted pumpkin seeds

Directions

1. Preheat the oven to 425° F/220° C.

2. Combine all the ingredients in the Wonder Cooker's Roaster Pan and toss.

3. Place the Roaster Pan in the oven and roast at 425° F/220° C until tender (about 1 hr.).

Eric's Tip: You can turn this into a hearty vegetarian taco filling by tossing with cumin and paprika and topping with your traditional taco garnishes.

Cheesy Cauliflower Pilaf

Ingredients

3 heads cauliflower

3 tbsp. butter

2 cups chopped onion

3 cloves garlic, chopped

1 cup chicken broth

½ tsp. salt

¼ tsp. ground black pepper

2 tbsp. thyme

¼ cup white wine

½ cup half & half

½ cup grated Parmesan cheese

6 oz grated Swiss cheese

Directions

1. Chop the cauliflower in a food processor until rice sized.

2. Place the Wonder Cooker's Roaster Pan on the stove top. Melt the butter in the Roaster Pan over medium heat and then sauté the onion and garlic for 2 mins.

3. Stir in the cauliflower and chicken broth. Cover with the Glass Lid and cook for 10 mins., stirring occasionally.

4. Remove the Glass Lid, reduce the temperature to low, and stir in the salt, ground black pepper, thyme, white wine, half & half, and Parmesan and Swiss cheese until the cheese melts.

Eric's Tip: Try making an Indian-style pilaf with curry sauce, cilantro, and baby spinach.

Creamed Kale

Ingredients

3 tsp. salt, divided

2 lb kale

4 tbsp. butter

3 cloves garlic, minced

1 Vidalia onion

2 tsp. ground black pepper

1 tsp. grated nutmeg

¼ cup flour

4 cups heavy cream

1 cup mozzarella cheese

½ cup Parmesan cheese

Directions

1. Preheat the oven to 350° F/175° C.

2. Place the Wonder Cooker's Roaster Pan on the stove top. Fill the Roaster Pan halfway with water and 2 tsp. salt and bring to a boil over high heat.

3. Add the kale, boil for 1 min., and let the kale cool. When cool, squeeze the water out and chop the kale roughly. Reserve the cooked kale.

4. Lower the heat to medium. Melt the butter with the garlic, onion, ground black pepper, ½ tsp. nutmeg, and 1 tsp. salt in the Roaster Pan and cook for 6–8 mins.

5. Mix in the flour and cook for 2–3 mins.

6. Add the heavy cream and cook until boiling.

7. Add the mozzarella cheese and cook for 6–8 mins.

8. Remove from the heat and mix in the kale.

9. Sprinkle with Parmesan cheese and ½ tsp. nutmeg.

10. Transfer the Roaster Pan to the oven and bake at 350° F/175° C until browned (30–45 mins.).

Eric's Tip: Adding in a half box of cooked penne and some rotisserie chicken before baking turns this side dish into the main course.

Spring Risotto

Ingredients

2 14.5-oz cartons of chicken broth

2 ½ cups water

3 tbsp. butter

8 oz zucchini, peeled & diced small

8 oz yellow squash, peeled & diced small

1 cup frozen peas, thawed

1 small onion, chopped

1 tsp. salt

¼ tsp. ground white pepper

2 tbsp. marjoram

1 ½ cups Arborio rice

½ cup white wine

¾ cup grated Parmesan cheese

Directions

1. Combine the broth and water in a bowl. Reserve the broth in the bowl.

2. Place the Wonder Cooker's Roaster Pan on the stove top. Melt the butter over medium-high heat and then add the zucchini and peas.

3. Cook for 5 mins. stirring often. Remove and reserve the vegetables.

4. Add the onion, salt, ground white pepper, and marjoram and then cook for 5 mins.

5. Add the rice and cook for 3 mins.

6. Add the wine. Cook until the rice absorbs all the wine.

7. Add 1 cup of the reserved broth to the rice and cook until it is absorbed. Repeat until all the broth has been used.

8. Remove the Roaster Pan from the heat and add the reserved vegetables and Parmesan cheese. Mix to combine.

Eric's Tip: I love many things about risotto, but my favorite is how you can form the leftovers into cakes and sauté them for a crispy treat.

Spanish Oven Rice

Ingredients

2 tbsp. olive oil

2 tbsp. shallots, chopped

2 cloves garlic, diced

1 red pepper, diced

2 cups white rice

1 tsp. salt

1 ½ tsp. turmeric

4 cups water

1 cup chicken broth

1 ½ cups frozen peas

¼ cup chopped cilantro

Directions

1. Preheat the oven to 350° F/175° C.

2. Place the Wonder Cooker's Roaster Pan on the stove top. Heat the olive oil over medium-high heat and then sauté the shallots and garlic for 2 mins.

3. Add the red pepper and cook for 1 min.

4. Add the white rice, salt, turmeric, water, chicken broth, peas, and cilantro and stir to combine.

5. Transfer the Roaster Pan to the oven and bake at 350° F/175° C for 50–55 mins.

Eric's Tip: You can serve this rice with literally anything! Roasted chicken, sautéed fish, grilled beef, fresh seafood, and local vegetables! Don't forget the shaved manchego cheese on top.

Crispy Bacon Brussels Sprouts

SERVES 10–12

Ingredients

4 slices bacon, chopped

2 tbsp. butter

3 cloves garlic, smashed

½ tsp. salt

½ tsp. ground black pepper

1 48-oz bag Brussels sprouts

¼ cup Parmesan cheese, grated

1 tbsp. olive oil

2 tbsp. lemon juice

zest of 1 lemon

Directions

1. Preheat the oven to 375° F/190° C.

2. Place the Wonder Cooker's Roaster Pan on the stove top. Cook the bacon in the Roaster Pan over medium heat until golden brown. Remove and reserve the bacon.

3. Discard all but 1 tbsp. of the bacon grease in the Roaster Pan.

4. Add the butter to the remaining bacon grease and sauté the garlic with the salt and ground black pepper.

5. Add the Brussels sprouts, Parmesan cheese, olive oil, and lemon juice and zest. Transfer the Roaster Pan to the oven and bake at 375° F/190° C for 35–40 mins.

Eric's Tip: This recipe makes a great omelet filling for your next Sunday brunch.

FISH & SEAFOOD

Fried Green Beans with Garlic Lime Dip

Jalapeño & Bacon Wonton Poppers

Salt & Vinegar Chicken Wings

Shrimp & Pork Toast

Portobello Rockefeller

Chicken Tender Romano

Chipotle Chicken Egg Rolls with Lime Dipping Sauce

Sweet & Spicy Party Mix

Onion-Fried Pickle Spears

Avocado Toast

Bangkok BBQ Chicken Wings

Ingredients

Eric's Special Tartar Sauce

1 cup mayonnaise

2 scallions, sliced thinly

1 tbsp. chopped parsley

1 tsp. Dijon mustard

1 tsp. lemon zest

2 tsp. lemon juice

1 clove garlic, grated

———

5 qts. canola oil

1 cup flour

½ tsp. ground black pepper

1 tsp. salt

½ tsp. onion powder

1 tsp. paprika

1 ½ lb cod fillets, skinned, boned & cut diagonally into 1-in. strips

6 oz beer

¼ cup water

½ cup cornstarch

Spicy Chips

1 tbsp. chili powder

¼ tsp. chipotle pepper powder

½ tsp. cumin

1 tsp. paprika

½ tsp. onion powder

1 tsp. salt

2 Idaho potatoes, sliced thinly

Fried & Beer-Battered Cod

with Eric's Special Tartar Sauce & Spicy Chips

Directions

1. Combine the sauce ingredients in a small bowl. Reserve the sauce in the refrigerator.

2. Place the Wonder Cooker's Roaster Pan on the stove top. Heat the canola oil over medium-high heat until the temperature reaches 325° F/160° C.

3. Combine the flour, ground black pepper, 1 tsp. salt, ½ tsp. onion powder, and 1 tsp. paprika in a glass bowl. Add the beer and water and mix to make a smooth batter.

4. Dust the cod fillets with the cornstarch, dip in the batter, shake off the excess batter, and fry the fillets in the Roaster Pan until golden brown (5–8 mins.). Drain on paper towels.

5. Combine the chili powder, chipotle pepper powder, cumin, 1 tsp. paprika, ½ tsp. onion powder, and 1 tsp. salt in a separate small bowl to make the seasoning mix.

6. Add the potatoes to the Roaster Pan and fry until golden brown and then toss with the seasoning mix.

7. Serve the finished fillets with the chips and sauce.

Eric's Tip: Don't judge me on this, but I love to wrap the fish, tartar sauce, lettuce, tomato, and chips in a tortilla for an amazing crunchy fish burrito.

Salmon Burgers

with Eric's Dill Sauce

Ingredients

Eric's Dill Sauce

⅓ cup Greek yogurt

¼ cup mayonnaise

1 ½ tsp. horseradish

1 tsp. lemon juice

1 tsp. lemon zest

1 tbsp. chopped fresh dill

———

2 lb salmon, skin removed & meat chopped

2 cups panko breadcrumbs

2 eggs

1 red bell pepper, diced finely

3 scallions, sliced thinly

2 tbsp. chopped parsley

2 tbsp. lemon juice

zest of ½ lemon

½ tsp. salt

¼ tsp. ground black pepper

½ tsp. crushed red pepper flakes

¼ cup canola oil

7 brioche buns, cut in half

Directions

1. Combine the Eric's Dill Sauce ingredients in a small bowl. Reserve the sauce in the refrigerator.

2. Combine the salmon, panko breadcrumbs, eggs, red bell pepper, scallions, parsley, lemon juice and zest, salt, ground black pepper, and red pepper flakes in a separate bowl. Form into seven 6-oz patties.

3. Place the Wonder Cooker's Grill Pan on the stove top. Heat the canola oil over medium heat and then grill each side of the patties for 5–7 mins.

4. Top the lower halves of the brioche buns with the patties, then Eric's Dill Sauce, and finally the top halves of the buns.

Eric's Tip: For a little twist on this recipe, I'll place this salmon burger in the middle of two pieces of Texas toast and some cheddar for an awesome grilled cheese.

Tuna Burgers with Avocado Aioli

Ingredients

Aioli

1 avocado, peeled & chopped

¼ cup mayonnaise

juice of ½ lime

½ tsp. salt

¼ tsp. ground black pepper

Burgers

2 lb tuna steaks, cut in cubes

4 scallions, sliced thinly

1 tbsp. toasted sesame oil

1 ½ tbsp. sweet soy sauce

½ tsp. salt

¼ tsp. ground black pepper

1 tbsp. lime zest

juice of 1 lime

1 tbsp. olive oil

——

6 hamburger buns, cut in half

Directions

1. Mash the aioli ingredients together to combine. Reserve the aioli in a bowl in the refrigerator.

2. Combine the burger ingredients in a food processor and pulse 3–4 times. Be sure not to overprocess.

3. Form the mixture into six 6-oz patties.

4. Place the Wonder Cooker's Grill Pan on the stove top. Preheat the Grill Pan over medium-high heat and cook each side of the patties for 4–5 mins.

5. Serve the burgers on the hamburger buns with the aioli.

Eric's Tip: If I'm having guests over, I'll make smaller 3-oz patties to put on slider buns for an easy finger food.

Maryland-Style Shrimp Étouffée

SERVES 6

Ingredients

3 sticks butter, divided

¼ cup flour

1 cup chopped onion

½ cup chopped green bell pepper

½ cup chopped celery

¼ tsp. salt

¼ tsp. ground black pepper

1 tbsp. fish seasoning

1 tsp. ground cayenne pepper

1 ½ lb andouille sausage

2 qts. water

1 tbsp. chicken base

¼ cup chopped parsley

tops of 1 bunch scallions, chopped

3 lb medium shrimp

Directions

1. Place the Wonder Cooker's Roaster Pan on the stove top. Preheat the Roaster Pan over medium heat, melt 1 stick of butter, add the flour, and cook for 5–7 mins to make a roux. Remove the roux and reserve in a bowl.

2. Melt 1 stick of butter and then sauté the onions, green bell pepper, and celery until translucent. Add the salt, ground black pepper, fish seasoning, and ground cayenne pepper.

3. Add the sausage and cook for 5 mins.

4. Add the water and chicken base, raise the heat level to bring to a boil, and then lower the heat level to simmer for 20 mins.

5. Mix in the roux, whisking constantly while raising the heat level to bring back to a boil.

6. Add the parsley, scallions, and shrimp and then lower the heat level to simmer until the shrimp are cooked (about 10 mins.).

7. Mix in the last stick of butter.

8. Serve over steamed rice.

Eric's Tip: Étouffée comes from the French word étouffer, which means "to smother." I love to smother a baked potato or cheesy biscuits with this étouffée.

Baked Fish

with Creamy Spinach Risotto

Ingredients

1 tbsp. olive oil

1 clove garlic, crushed

2 scallions, chopped

10 oz Arborio rice

2 ½ cups vegetable stock

1 ½ cups heavy cream

1 tsp. salt, divided

¼ tsp. ground black pepper

12 oz skinless white fish

½ cup white wine

juice of ½ lemon

4 oz young-leaf spinach

4 oz frozen peas

½ tsp. ground white pepper

3 tbsp. grated Parmesan cheese

Directions

1. Preheat the oven to 350° F/175° C.

2. Place the Wonder Cooker's Roaster Pan on the stove top. Heat the olive oil over high heat and then sauté the garlic, scallions, and rice for 2 mins.

3. Add the vegetable stock and heavy cream, bring to a boil, and then lower the heat to simmer for 10 mins.

4. Season the fish with the ground black pepper and ½ tsp. salt.

5. Remove the Roaster Pan from the heat and place the fish on top of the risotto.

6. Cover the Roaster Pan with the Grill Pan, transfer to the oven, and bake at 350° F/175° C for 15 mins.

7. Remove from the oven and stir in the lemon juice, spinach, and peas, breaking up the fish into small pieces.

8. Let sit for 2 mins., season with the salt and ground white pepper, and sprinkle with the Parmesan cheese.

Eric's Tip: I love to turn this recipe into a rich brunch dish by using salmon and topping each bowl with a poached egg drizzled with truffle oil and chopped chives.

Sriracha Apricot Mahi Mahi

with Roasted Grape Tomatoes

Ingredients

½ cup apricot preserves

juice of ½ lemon

¼ tsp. cumin

½ tsp. salt

¼ tsp. ground black pepper

1 tsp. sriracha sauce

2 oranges, sliced thickly

5 5-oz mahi mahi fillets

1 cup tri-colored grape tomatoes

1 tsp. olive oil

¼ tsp. salt

¼ tsp. ground black pepper

2 tsp. chopped chives, for garnish

Directions

1. Preheat the oven to 400° F/205° C. Lightly spray the Wonder Cooker's Grill Pan with cooking spray.

2. Combine the apricot preserves, lemon juice, cumin, salt, ground black pepper, and sriracha sauce in a small bowl. Microwave for 1 min. to melt and complete the marinade.

3. Arrange the orange slices on the bottom of the Grill Pan. Place the mahi mahi fillets on top of the oranges.

4. Combine the tomatoes, olive oil, salt, and ground black pepper in a separate small bowl. Toss the tomatoes along the sides of the fillets.

5. Brush the marinade on the fillets. Place the Grill Pan in the oven and bake at 400° F/205° C until the fillets are cooked (about 10 mins.).

6. Garnish with the chives.

Eric's Tip: This dish goes hand in hand with a curry coconut-flavored jasmine rice. Don't forget the sautéed spinach!

SERVES 6

Honey BBQ-Glazed
Sesame Salmon

Ingredients

½ cup BBQ sauce

½ tbsp. sriracha sauce

1 tbsp. rice wine vinegar

⅓ cup honey

1 clove garlic, minced

1 tsp. grated ginger

6 salmon fillets

2 tbsp. sesame seeds

½ cup sliced scallions

Directions

1. Preheat the oven to 425° F/220° C. Lightly spray the Wonder Cooker's Grill Pan with cooking spray.

2. Combine the BBQ sauce, sriracha sauce, rice wine vinegar, honey, garlic, and ginger in a small bowl to make the marinade.

3. Place the salmon fillets in the Grill Pan and brush with the marinade.

4. Place the Grill Pan in the oven and bake at 425° F/220° C for 5 mins.

5. Brush with the marinade and cook at 425° F/220° C until the fillets are cooked through (about 10 mins).

6. Brush with any remaining marinade and broil for 2–3 mins.

7. Sprinkle with the sesame seeds and scallions.

Eric's Tip: I like to cool the salmon in the fridge and then flake it into chunks. Adding some mayonnaise, a light squeeze of lime, and a pinch of fresh cilantro will give you a delicious salmon salad.

Grilled Scallops
with a Lemony Salsa Verde

SERVES 6

Ingredients

Salsa Verde

peel of ½ lemon, chopped

zest of 1 lemon

½ cup cilantro, chopped

½ cup parsley, chopped

2 cloves garlic, chopped

1 shallot, chopped

1 ½ tbsp. capers, chopped

½ tsp. Kosher salt

¼ tsp. ground black pepper

½ cup olive oil

———

2 tbsp. olive oil

1 ½ lb U12 scallops

Directions

1. Combine the salsa verde ingredients in a bowl and let sit for 15 mins.

2. Place the Wonder Cooker's Roaster Pan on the stove top. Heat 2 tbsp. olive oil over medium-high heat.

3. Grill each side of the scallops for 3–5 mins. per side.

4. Serve with the salsa verde.

Eric's Tip: I love to grill and then cool these scallops to use as a refreshing salad topper. Just toss baby arugula and shaved fennel with the salsa verde and add the scallops.

Ingredients

2 1-lb whole branzinos, cleaned

4 sprigs cilantro

1 lime, sliced thinly

½ cup chopped cilantro

½ cup chopped mint

¼ cup lime juice

1 tbsp. lime zest

1 1-in. piece fresh ginger, peeled & grated

1 tsp. sugar

1 red chili with seeds, sliced thinly

1 tsp. kosher salt

⅓ cup olive oil

Orzo Salad

2 tsp. lemon juice

1 tsp. salt

1 tsp. ground black pepper

1 tsp. minced shallots

1 tsp. honey

¼ cup olive oil

1 cup cherry tomatoes, cut in half

¼ cup sliced Kalamata olives

¼ cup crumbled feta cheese

¼ cup chopped parsley

1 cup orzo, cooked al dente, drained & cooled

Grilled Branzino

with Mediterranean Orzo Salad

Directions

1. Preheat the oven to 350° F/175° C.

2. Stuff the cavity of each branzino with 2 sprigs of cilantro and 2 lime slices.

3. Place the Wonder Cooker's Grill Pan on the stove top. Preheat the Grill Pan over medium-high heat.

4. Process the chopped cilantro, mint, lime juice and zest, ginger, sugar, red chili, salt, and olive oil in a food chopper to make the cilantro mixture.

5. Brush the branzinos with the cilantro mixture and grill each side of the branzinos in the Grill Pan for 5–7 mins.

6. Transfer the Grill Pan to the oven and bake at 350° F/175° C for 10 mins.

7. Process the lemon juice, salt, ground black pepper, shallots, and honey in a food chopper to combine. Slowly add the olive oil to finish the dressing.

8. Combine the tomatoes, Kalamata olives, feta cheese, parsley, orzo, and dressing in a bowl to finish the orzo salad.

9. Serve the branzinos with the salad.

Eric's Tip: If you can't find branzino, you can easily substitute red snapper fillets in this recipe. I also love to experiment with the salad. I'll use farro, couscous, or brown rice instead of the orzo for a nuttier flavor.

Seafood Bake

Ingredients

6 tbsp. butter

6 tbsp. flour

5 cups heavy cream

2 tbsp. sherry

½ tsp. salt

¼ tsp. ground white pepper

¼ cup shredded Parmesan cheese

1 ½ lb red potatoes, sliced

2 medium onions, sliced

1 ½ lb 21–25 shrimp, peeled & deveined

1 lb scallops, cleaned

1 ½ lb cod fish

¼ tsp. paprika

2 cups roughly crushed oyster crackers

2 tbsp. butter, melted

Directions

1. Preheat the oven to 350° F/175° C.

2. Place the Wonder Cooker's Roaster Pan on the stove top. Melt 6 tbsp. butter over medium-high heat and then add the flour to make a roux.

3. Slowly add the heavy cream and stir until the mixture thickens.

4. Add the sherry, salt, ground white pepper, and Parmesan cheese. Mix to combine.

5. Remove the Roaster Pan from the heat and layer in the potatoes, onions, shrimp, and scallops. Top with the cod.

6. Sprinkle with the paprika and oyster crackers and drizzle with the melted butter.

7. Cover the Roaster Pan with the Grill Pan, place in the oven, and bake at 350° F/175° C for 20 mins.

8. Remove the Grill Pan and bake at 350° F/175° C for an additional 15 mins.

Eric's Tip: I enjoy adding fresh crab, corn, bay seasoning, and a good spoonful of whole-grain mustard for a Maryland-style bake.

Steamed Mussels

in Chorizo Saffron Broth

SERVES 6

Ingredients

2 tbsp. olive oil

2 garlic cloves, chopped

1 large shallot, sliced thinly

1 large leek, sliced

1 tsp. crushed red pepper flakes

4 chorizo links, sliced

6 cups chicken broth

1 cup dry sherry

¼ tsp. saffron

1 tbsp. smoked paprika

4 oz mussels

½ cup parsley leaves

Directions

1. Place the Wonder Cooker's Roaster Pan on the stove top. Heat the olive oil over medium heat. Add the garlic, shallot, leek, and crushed red pepper flakes and cook for 2 mins.

2. Add the chorizo and cook for 5 min.

3. Add the chicken broth, sherry, saffron, and paprika and cook for 5 mins.

4. Add the mussels, cover with the Grill Pan, and cook until the mussels open (about 3 mins.).

5. Garnish with the parsley.

Eric's Tip: Saffron can sometimes be hard to find or a little on the pricy side. If I don't have it in my spice cabinet, I'll add 1 tsp. ground turmeric. You'll get a beautiful golden color in the sauce with a similar flavor profile.

MEATS

Eric's Dry Rub Brisket

Grilled Ranch-Style Flank Steak

Roast Pork Loin with Apple & Sauerkraut

Fennel-Crusted Roast Beef

Gorgonzola-Stuffed Filet of Beef
with Caramelized Onions & Mushrooms

Shandy-Braised Pork Shoulder

Braised Lamb Shanks

Spiced Apricot Lamb

Spinach- & Prosciutto-Stuffed Pork Loin

Pork Osso Bucco

Korean-Style Short Ribs

Eric's Spicy BBQ Ribs

Osso Bucco

Braciole

Apricot-Glazed Baked Ham

Eric's Dry Rub Brisket

Ingredients

Coleslaw

½ head cabbage, shredded

1 carrot, shredded

½ red pepper, minced

¼ red onion, minced

½ cup mayonnaise

1 tbsp. apple cider vinegar

1 tsp. sugar

Rub

1 tsp. granulated garlic

1 tsp. granulated onion

1 tbsp. dried thyme

3 tbsp. brown sugar

1 tsp. liquid smoke

1 tsp. paprika

2 tsp. hot chili powder

1 tsp. ground black pepper

1 tbsp. sea salt

6 lb brisket, trimmed

1 cup BBQ sauce

Directions

1. Combine the coleslaw ingredients in a bowl. Cover the bowl with plastic wrap and place in the refrigerator.

2. Preheat the oven to 325° F/160° C.

3. Combine the rub ingredients in a separate bowl. Coat the brisket with the rub.

4. Place the brisket in the Wonder Cooker's Roaster Pan.

5. Place the Roaster Pan in the oven and roast at 325° F/160° C until tender (about 5 hrs.).

6. Slice and serve with the coleslaw and BBQ sauce or make sliders.

Eric's Tip: When making a brisket sandwich, there is a big debate over sliced or chopped brisket. I prefer to go both ways on the same sandwich. Just make sure you top with slaw.

Grilled Ranch-Style Flank Steak

SERVES 6

Ingredients

Rub

1 tsp. onion powder

1 tsp. garlic powder

2 tsp. mustard powder

1 tsp. sea salt

½ tsp. ground black pepper

1 tsp. dry chives

1 tsp. dry parsley

1 tsp. dry dill

———

2 tsp. apple cider vinegar

1 2-lb flank steak

2 tbsp. olive oil

Directions

1. Combine the rub ingredients in a small bowl and mix. Coat both sides of the steak with the rub.

2. Drizzle the apple cider vinegar on each side of the steak.

3. Preheat the Grill Pan on the stove top over high heat.

4. Preheat the oven 400° F/205° C.

5. Add the olive oil to the Grill Pan and then grill each side of the steak (about 2 ½ mins. per side).

6. Transfer the Grill Pan to the oven and cook at 400° F/205° C until the internal temperature of the steak reaches 120° F/50° C (about 10 mins.).

7. Let rest for 5 mins. before slicing.

Eric's Tip: If you're looking for a more economical cut of meat for this recipe, you can get a sirloin or London broil. Just cut into 1-in. slices and give them a quick pound with a meat tenderizer.

Roast Pork Loin

with Apple & Sauerkraut

SERVES 12

Ingredients

Pork Rub

1 tbsp. caraway seeds

1 tsp. sea salt

1 tsp. ground black pepper

1 tbsp. minced dry onion

1 tbsp. paprika

———

1 8-lb pork loin, cut in half

¼ cup olive oil

2 shallots, minced

1 32-oz can sauerkraut

1 12-oz bottle hard cider

1 12-oz lager beer

1 18-oz jar chicken gravy

1 cup applesauce

3 green apples, sliced

1 large onion, sliced

½ cup brown sugar

1 stick butter

Directions

1. Combine the pork rub ingredients in a small bowl and mix. Coat the pork loins with the rub.

2. Place the Wonder Cooker's Roaster Pan on the stove top. Heat the olive oil over high heat. Brown the pork loins on both sides. Remove and reserve the pork loins.

3. Preheat the oven to 375° F/190° C.

4. Add the shallot to the Roaster Pan and cook for 2 mins.

5. Combine the sauerkraut, hard cider, lager beer, chicken gravy, and applesauce in the Roaster Pan.

6. Place the pork loins in the Roaster Pan and top with the apple and onion.

7. Bring to a boil and then turn off the heat.

8. Cover the Roaster Pan with the Grill Pan, transfer to the oven, and bake at 375° F/190° C for 2 ½ hrs.

9. Remove and slice the pork.

10. Transfer the Roaster Pan, without a lid, to the stove top. Melt the butter over medium heat and cook until the sauerkraut is reduced by one third.

11. Serve the pork loins with the sauerkraut.

Eric's Tip: I'll make this rub in a larger quantity and use the rub to season everything from chicken, to burgers, to grilled shrimp.

Fennel-Crusted Roast Beef

SERVES

Ingredients

3 tbsp. olive oil

1 4-lb eye round roast beef

¼ cup Dijon mustard

Fennel Rub

3 tbsp. ground fennel

½ tbsp. garlic powder

½ tbsp. onion powder

1 tbsp. sea salt

½ tbsp. ground black pepper

———

1 bulb fresh fennel, sliced

1 onion, sliced

Gravy

3 tbsp. butter

3 tbsp. flour

½ cup red wine

2 cups beef stock

1 bay leaf

3 sprigs thyme

¼ tsp. ground black pepper

Directions

1. Preheat the oven to 400° F/205° C.

2. Place the Wonder Cooker's Roaster Pan on the stove top. Heat the olive oil over high heat and sear the roast on all sides.

3. Remove the Roaster Pan from the heat and brush the roast with the mustard.

4. Combine the fennel rub ingredients in a bowl. Coat the roast with the rub.

5. Add the sliced fennel and onion to the Roaster Pan.

6. Transfer the Roaster Pan to the oven and roast at 400° F/205° C until the roast reaches an internal temperature of 120° F/50° C (about 1 ¼ hrs.). Remove and reserve the roast.

7. Transfer the Roaster Pan to the stove top. Melt the butter over medium heat.

8. Add the flour and mix until creamy.

9. Stir in the red wine and beef stock until combined.

10. Add the bay leaf, thyme, and ground black pepper. Cook over low heat for 20 mins. to finish the gravy.

11. Slice the roast and serve with the gravy.

Eric's Tip: I'll dice up the leftover beef, mix it with veggies, and top with mashed potatoes for a hearty shepherd's pie.

Gorgonzola-Stuffed Filet of Beef

with Caramelized Onions & Mushrooms

SERVES 6

Ingredients

3 lb center cut filet of beef

¾ lb Gorgonzola cheese, sliced

2 shallots, minced

½ cup extra virgin olive oil

½ tbsp. sea salt

4 sprigs of thyme

½ tbsp. ground black pepper

¼ cup balsamic vinegar

Caramelized Onions & Mushrooms

¼ cup olive oil

3 onions, sliced

2 lb baby bella mushrooms, sliced

4 sprigs thyme

½ tbsp. ground black pepper

¾ cup brown stock

3 tbsp. butter

2 tbsp. Worcestershire sauce

2 tbsp. balsamic vinegar

Directions

1. Use a boning knife to make a hole in the filet lengthwise. Take a steel or wooden dowel and enlarge the hole.

2. Stuff the filet with the Gorgonzola cheese.

3. Mix the shallot, extra virgin olive oil, salt, thyme, ½ tbsp. ground black pepper, and ¼ cup balsamic vinegar in the Wonder Cooker's Roaster Pan to make the marinade.

4. Marinate the filet in the marinade for 40 mins.

5. Preheat the oven to 400° F/205° C.

6. Place the Grill Pan on the stove top. Remove the filet from the marinade and sear all sides over high heat.

7. Transfer the Grill Pan to the oven and cook at 400° F/205° C until the filet reaches the desired doneness.

8. Clean the marinade out of the Roaster Pan and then place the Roaster Pan on the stove top. Heat the olive oil over medium heat and caramelize the onion and mushroom.

9. Add the thyme and ½ tbsp. ground black pepper followed by the brown stock.

10. Add the butter, Worcestershire sauce, and 2 tbsp. balsamic vinegar to the mushrooms; turn off the heat; and stir.

11. Slice the filet and serve on a platter with the onions and mushrooms.

Eric's Tip: The perfect sides to this filet of beef are smashed bliss potatoes with cream, butter, and caramelized leeks.

149

Shandy-Braised Pork Shoulder

SERVES 8

Ingredients

1 8-lb pork shoulder, boneless

1 14.9-oz shandy beer

½ cup orange marmalade

2 onions, diced

8 cloves garlic

2 cups ketchup

½ long hot red pepper

2 tbsp. dry mustard

1 tbsp. sea salt

rind of 1 lemon

1 tsp. ground black pepper

8 slider rolls

Directions

1. Preheat the oven to 350° F/175° C.

2. Place the Wonder Cooker's Roaster Pan on the stove top.

3. Combine the pork shoulder, shandy beer, orange marmalade, onion, ketchup, red pepper, mustard, salt, lemon rind, and ground black pepper in the Roaster Pan.

4. Bring to a boil over high heat.

5. Cover the Roaster Pan with the Grill Pan, transfer to the oven, and cook at 350° F/175° C for 3 hrs.

6. Remove from the oven and transfer to the stove top.

7. Simmer over medium-low heat for 45–60 mins.

8. Shred the meat and serve on the slider rolls.

Eric's Tip: I love to serve this pork Cuban style by pairing it with black beans and yellow rice!

Braised Lamb Shanks

SERVES 6

Ingredients

¼ cup olive oil

6 lamb shanks

1 onion, minced

4 carrots

1 shallot, minced

6 cloves garlic

1 tbsp. sea salt

1 tbsp. ground black pepper

6 baby leek greens, chopped

2 tbsp. tomato paste

2 cups red wine

3 cups brown stock

1 bay leaf

1 sprig rosemary

Directions

1. Place the Wonder Cooker's Roaster Pan on the stove top. Preheat over high heat.

2. Add the olive oil and brown all sides of the shanks. Remove and reserve the shanks.

3. Preheat the oven to 350° F/175° C.

4. Reduce the heat to medium; add the onion, carrots, shallot, garlic, salt, ground black pepper, and leek greens; and cook for 5 mins.

5. Add the tomato paste and stir to combine.

6. Place the shanks on top and then add the red wine and brown stock.

7. Add the bay leaf and rosemary.

8. Cover the Roaster Pan with the Glass Lid, transfer to the oven, and bake at 350° F/175° C until tender and falling off the bone (about 3 hrs.).

9. Serve the shanks on a platter.

Eric's Tip: This dish is so decadent and rich that I love to serve it with a hearty mushroom risotto topped with crumbled Gorgonzola cheese.

Spiced Apricot Lamb

Ingredients

Pesto

5 cloves garlic, minced

½ bunch of mint

3 sprigs rosemary, leaves only

1 tsp. oregano

1 tsp. brown mustard

1 tsp. sea salt

1 tsp. ground black pepper

10 dried apricots

juice of 1 lemon

½ cup water

¼ cup extra virgin olive oil

———

4 lb boneless leg of lamb, butterflied

Directions

1. Preheat the oven to 400° F/205° C.

2. Combine all the pesto ingredients food processor and make a paste.

3. Rub the inside of the lamb with the pesto.

4. Roll the lamb and tie it.

5. Place the lamb in the Wonder Cooker's Roaster Pan.

6. Place the Roaster Pan in the oven and roast at 400° F/205° C for 30 mins.

7. Lower the oven temperature to 350° F/175° C and roast until the internal temperature of the lamb reaches 135° F/55° C (about 1 hr.).

8. Let rest for 20 mins. before slicing.

Eric's Tip: This dish makes an excellent upscale gyro. Slice the lamb thinly and top with lettuce, tomato, onion, and tzatziki sauce.

Spinach- & Prosciutto-Stuffed

Pork Loin

Ingredients

6 tbsp. olive oil, divided

2 cloves garlic, sliced thinly

10 oz spinach

Cream Cheese Filling

1 oz cream cheese

2 cloves garlic, minced

1 sprig rosemary, chopped

4 sprigs thyme, chopped

2 sage leaves, chopped

2 tbsp. heavy cream

¼ tsp. sea salt

¼ tsp. ground black pepper

___

4 lb pork loin, trimmed
& butterflied

1 tbsp. sea salt

1 tbsp. ground black pepper

6 slices prosciutto

Directions

1. Place the Wonder Cooker's Roaster Pan on the stove top. Heat 3 tbsp. olive oil over medium heat, add the garlic, and cook until slightly golden.

2. Add the spinach and cook until wilted and reduced. Remove and let cool. Once cool, drain the spinach.

3. Mix the cream cheese filling ingredients in a stand mixer until creamy.

4. Pound the pork on a cutting board to flatten slightly.

5. Place the prosciutto on three quarters of each pork loin.

6. Spread the cream cheese filling on each loin and top with the spinach.

7. Roll each pork loin, tie with butcher's twine, and then season with the salt and ground black pepper.

8. Preheat the oven to 350° F/175° C.

9. Place the Grill Pan on the stove top. Heat 3 tbsp. olive oil over high heat and sear the pork loins.

10. Transfer the Grill Pan to the oven and cook at 350° F/175° C until the pork reaches an internal temperature of 155° F/70° C (about 1 ½ hrs.).

11. Remove the pork and let rest for 15 mins.

12. Transfer the Grill Pan to the stove top. Bring the remaining liquid to a boil over high heat. Reduce the liquid to make a sauce.

13. Pour the sauce over the pork and serve.

Eric's Tip: The pork loin will release juice during cooking. When you reduce the liquid, the cream cheese will make the sauce creamy.

Pork Osso Bucco

Ingredients

4 pork shanks

1 tbsp. sea salt

1 tbsp. ground black pepper

¼ cup olive oil

1 large shallot, minced

3 cloves garlic, minced

1 onion, diced small

3 carrots, diced small

3 celery stalks, diced small

2 tbsp. tomato paste

2 cups white wine

2 cups beef stock

½ cup dry vermouth

2 oranges, cut into 8 wedges

1 bay leaf

2 sprigs oregano

10 basil leaves

3 tbsp. chopped parsley

Directions

1. Season the pork shanks with the salt and ground black pepper.

2. Place the Wonder Cooker's Roaster Pan on the stove top. Heat the olive oil over high heat and then brown the shanks. Remove and reserve the shanks.

3. Preheat the oven to 350° F/175° C.

4. Add the shallot, garlic, onion, carrot, and celery and cook over medium heat for 4 mins.

5. Add the tomato paste and stir to combine.

6. Place the shanks back in the Roaster Pan.

7. Add the white wine, beef stock, vermouth, orange wedges, bay leaf, oregano, basil, and parsley and bring to a boil over high heat.

8. Cover the Roaster Pan with the Glass Lid, transfer to the oven, and bake at 350° F/175° C until the meat is tender and falling off the bone (about 2 ½ hrs.).

9. Remove and reserve the shanks.

10. Transfer the Roaster Pan to the stove top. Reduce the liquid over high heat until slightly thickened to make the sauce.

11. Serve the shanks with the sauce.

Eric's Tip: Sometimes, pork shanks are hard to find. As an alternative, cut a boneless pork butt into 6 large chunks. Then, continue with the directions.

Korean-Style Short Ribs

SERVES 10

Ingredients

¼ cup canola oil

8 lb boneless short ribs

1 tbsp. sea salt

1 tbsp. ground black pepper

Sauce

8 cloves garlic, minced

1 onion, diced small

2 bunches scallions, chopped

3 carrots, diced small

1 tsp. red pepper flakes

2 tbsp. fresh ginger, minced

½ cup sweet soy sauce

⅔ cup brown sugar

⅔ cup rice wine

1 tbsp. sesame oil

1 cup brown stock

¼ cup rice wine vinegar

Directions

1. Place the Wonder Cooker's Roaster Pan on the stove top. Heat the canola oil over high heat.

2. Season the ribs with the salt and ground black pepper.

3. Brown the ribs in the Roaster Pan.

4. Remove the ribs and sauté the garlic, onion, scallion, carrot, red pepper flakes, and ginger for 3–5 mins.

5. Preheat the oven to 350° F/175° C.

6. Add the ribs, soy sauce, brown sugar, rice wine, sesame oil, brown stock, and rice wine vinegar to the Roaster Pan.

7. Cover the Roaster Pan with the Glass Lid, transfer to the oven, and bake at 350° F/175° C until the meat is fork tender (about 3 hrs.).

8. Serve with jasmine rice.

Eric's Tip: These short ribs and rice make amazing tacos. Just top with the traditional pickled vegetables and fresh cilantro!

Eric's Spicy BBQ Ribs

Ingredients

Rub

1 tbsp. onion powder

1 tbsp. garlic powder

1 tbsp. cumin

1 tbsp. coriander

1 tbsp. sea salt

1 tbsp. paprika

½ tbsp. ground black pepper

——

3 full racks baby back ribs, cut in half

BBQ Sauce

3 tbsp. canola oil

1 onion, diced

1 red pepper, diced

2 cloves garlic, minced

1 7-oz can chipotle peppers in sauce

1 ½ cups ketchup

¾ cup brown sugar

¼ cup apple cider vinegar

¼ cup Dijon mustard

½ cup molasses

2 cups enchilada sauce

Directions

1. Preheat the oven to 300° F/150° C.

2. Combine all the rub ingredients in a bowl. Coat both sides of the ribs with the rub.

3. Place 3 half racks of ribs on the Wonder Cooker's Grill Pan and 3 half racks of ribs in the Roaster Pan.

4. Place both Pans in the oven and cook at 300° F/150° C for 5 hrs.

5. Place all the ribs in the Grill Pan. Reserve the ribs in the Grill Pan.

6. Place the Roaster Pan on the stove top. Heat the canola oil over medium heat and then sweat the onion and red pepper.

7. Add the onion, red pepper, garlic, chipotle peppers, ketchup, brown sugar, apple cider vinegar, mustard, molasses, and enchilada sauce and cook for 20 mins to complete the BBQ sauce. Toss the ribs with the BBQ sauce.

8. Clean the excess sauce out of the Roaster Pan and move 3 half racks of ribs to the Roaster Pan.

9. Transfer both Pans to the oven and cook at 300° F/150° C for 15 mins.

Eric's Tip: This recipe also works well with a boneless pork shoulder if ribs are not available.

Osso Bucco

Ingredients

4 large veal shanks

1 tbsp. sea salt

1 tbsp. ground black pepper

¼ cup olive oil

1 onion, diced small

2 stalks celery, diced small

3 carrots, diced small

5 cloves garlic, minced

3 cups tomato purée

1 bay leaf

2 cups brown stock

rind of ½ lemon

3 sprigs thyme

1 sprig rosemary

3 tbsp. unsalted butter

½ cup pesto

Directions

1. Season the veal shanks with the salt and ground black pepper.

2. Place the Wonder Cooker's Roaster Pan on the stove top. Heat the olive oil over high heat and then brown all sides of the shanks. Remove and reserve the shanks.

3. Preheat the oven to 350° F/175° C.

4. Add the onion, celery, carrot, and garlic and cook over medium heat for 4 mins.

5. Add the tomato purée and stir to combine.

6. Place the shanks back in the Roaster Pan.

7. Add the bay leaf, brown stock, lemon rind, thyme, and rosemary and bring to a boil.

8. Cover the Roaster Pan with the Grill Pan and bake at 350° F/175° C until the meat is tender and falling off the bone (about 2 ½ hrs.).

9. Remove from the oven and stir in the butter.

10. Serve the shanks with a dab of pesto on each plate.

Eric's Tip: My favorite way to serve this dish is with a classic soft polenta to soak up all that awesome sauce!

SERVES 8

Braciole

Ingredients

½ cup breadcrumbs

1 ½ tbsp. basil

2 cloves garlic, chopped

½ cup grated Parmesan cheese

¼ cup chopped parsley

½ cup pine nuts

7 tbsp. olive oil, divided

2 1 ½-lb flank steaks, pounded ¼ in. thick

14 slices provolone cheese

8 oz prosciutto, sliced

1 cup red wine

3 cups tomato sauce

½ tsp. salt

½ tsp. ground black pepper

1 bay leaf

Directions

1. Preheat the oven to 375° F/190° C.

2. Combine the breadcrumbs, basil, garlic, Parmesan cheese, parsley, pine nuts, and 5 tbsp. olive oil in a medium-size bowl to make the breadcrumb mixture.

3. Layer half the Provolone cheese and half the prosciutto on each steak.

4. Spread the breadcrumb mixture in an even layer on the two steaks.

5. Roll the steaks lengthwise into logs and secure with butcher's twine.

6. Place the Wonder Cooker's Roaster Pan on the stove top. Heat 2 tbsp. olive oil over medium-high heat and brown each side of the steak rolls.

7. Add the red wine, raise the heat level to bring to a boil, and then stir in the tomato sauce, salt, ground black pepper, and bay leaf.

8. Cover the Roaster Pan with the Grill Pan, place in the oven, and bake at 375° F/190° C for 30 mins.

9. Remove the Grill Pan and bake at 375° F/190° C for an additional 30 mins.

Eric's Tip: I love to slice this down into patties and serve it on a freshly baked ciabatta roll. Don't forget the roasted long hots!

Apricot-Glazed Baked Ham

SERVES 10

Ingredients

¾ cup apricot jam

2 tbsp. dry mustard

½ cup spicy brown mustard

½ shallot

1 sprig rosemary

3 tbsp. apple cider vinegar

1 can diced pineapple

½ cup pineapple juice

12 lb smoked ham, bone in

Directions

1. Preheat the oven to 375° F/190° C.

2. Preheat the Wonder Cooker's Roaster Pan over high heat on the stove top. Combine the apricot jam, dry mustard, spicy brown mustard, shallot, rosemary, apple cider vinegar, pineapple, and pineapple juice.

3. Reduce the contents of the Pan to make a glaze. Remove the glaze from the Pan and let cool.

4. Place the ham in the Roaster Pan and pour the glaze over the ham.

5. Transfer the Roaster Pan to the oven and cook at 375° F/190° C for 1 ½ hrs.

6. Slice the ham before serving.

Eric's Tip: Save the bone for split pea soup!

ONE-POT MEALS & CASSEROLES

Stewed Lemon Garlic Chicken Thighs

SERVES 8

Ingredients

8 leg and thigh quarters, trimmed

1 tsp. sea salt

1 tsp. ground black pepper

1 tsp. turmeric

1 tsp. paprika

¼ cup olive oil

1 cup white wine

1 onion, diced

15 cloves garlic

2 lemons, sliced

3 sprigs oregano

Directions

1. Preheat the oven to 375° F/190° C.

2. Rub the chicken with the salt, ground black pepper, turmeric, and paprika.

3. Place the Wonder Cooker's Roaster Pan on the stove top. Heat the olive oil over high heat and then sear the chicken thighs.

4. Top with the white wine, onion, garlic, lemon, and oregano.

5. Cover the Roaster Pan with the Glass Lid, place in the oven, and cook at 375° F/190° C for 1 hr.

Eric's Tip: There's something about a delicious roasted chicken served over garlicky greens that gets my mouth watering!

Chicken Pot Pie with Puff Pastry Top

SERVES 8

Ingredients

1 cup butter

1 cup flour

2 qts. chicken stock

2 tsp. salt

1 tsp. ground black pepper

2 tsp. thyme

1 tsp. turmeric

1 bay leaf

14 oz pearl onions

1 ½ lb baby potatoes, quartered

4 large carrots, diced large

4 stalks celery, diced

1 lb button mushrooms, quartered

3 lb chicken tenders

½ cup dry sherry

1 12-oz package of peas

¼ cup heavy cream

2 frozen puff pastry sheets, thawed

egg wash

Directions

1. Preheat the oven to 375° F/190° C.

2. Place the Wonder Cooker's Roaster Pan on the stove top. Melt the butter over medium heat, add the flour to make a roux, and cook for 3 mins.

3. Gradually add the chicken stock and cook until the mixture begins to thicken and bubble (8–10 mins.).

4. Add the salt, ground black pepper, thyme, turmeric, bay leaf, pearl onions, potatoes, carrots, celery, mushrooms, chicken tenders, and sherry. Continue cooking until the chicken tenders are cooked and the potatoes are tender (45–60 mins.).

5. Stir in the peas and cream.

6. Roll out the puff pastry sheets and place over the top of the Roaster Pan. Make slits in the center of the sheets and brush with egg wash.

7. Place the Roaster Pan in the oven and bake at 375° F/190° C until the pastry is golden (25–40 mins.).

Eric's Tip: If you're looking for a different top, try using premade biscuits instead of the puff pastry.

Chicken Fricassee

Ingredients

1 whole chicken, broken down

2 tsp. kosher salt

1 tsp. ground black pepper

4 tbsp. butter

1 onion, sliced

2 celery stalks, sliced diagonally

1 lb baby potatoes, quartered

10 oz button mushrooms, quartered

2 tbsp. flour

⅔ cup vermouth

3 cups chicken broth

1 can condensed cream of mushroom soup

4 sprigs thyme

4 sprigs parsley

1 bay leaf

Directions

1. Season the chicken with the salt and ground black pepper.

2. Place the Wonder Cooker's Roaster Pan on the stove top. Melt the butter over medium heat and then sear the chicken until brown all over (about 10 mins.). Remove and reserve the chicken.

3. Add the onions, celery, and potatoes and sauté for 8 mins.

4. Add the mushrooms and cook for 4 mins.

5. Stir in the flour and cook for 1 min.

6. Add the vermouth, chicken broth, and cream of mushroom soup.

7. Return the chicken to the Roaster Pan and add the thyme, parsley, and bay leaf.

8. Raise the heat level to bring to a boil, cover partially with the Glass Lid, and then lower the heat level to simmer for 1 ½ hrs.

Eric's Tip: I love this recipe because a few minor changes can make a different flavor profile. Swapping the mushroom soup for salsa, cilantro, and black beans will give it a southwestern flair.

Spaghetti Squash Casserole

SERVES 8

Ingredients

2 spaghetti squash, cut in half lengthwise & seeded

3 tbsp. olive oil, divided

4 mini leeks, sliced

2 cloves garlic, sliced

10 oz mushrooms, sliced

1 cup chopped spinach

1 tsp. salt

½ tsp. ground black pepper

¼ tsp. nutmeg

1 tbsp. oregano

1 cup shredded mozzarella cheese

Directions

1. Preheat the oven to 400° F/205° C.

2. Brush the cut ends of the squash with 1 tbsp. olive oil. Place in the Wonder Cooker's Roaster Pan.

3. Place the Roaster Pan in the oven and roast at 400° F/205° C for 40 mins.

4. Scrape out the inside of the squash with a fork. Reserve the inside of the squash in a bowl.

5. Transfer the Roaster Pan to the stove top. Heat 2 tbsp. olive oil over medium heat and then cook the leeks and garlic until soft.

6. Add the mushrooms and cook for 3 mins.

7. Remove the Roaster Pan from the heat. Add the spinach, salt, ground black pepper, nutmeg, and oregano. Mix in the squash to finish the vegetable mixture.

8. Lightly oil the Grill Pan and transfer the vegetable mixture onto it. Sprinkle with the mozzarella cheese.

9. Place the Grill Pan in the oven and bake at 400° F/205° C until the cheese melts (about 30 mins.).

Eric's Tip: Layering the vegetables between precooked pasta sheets before baking makes a great lasagna!

Broccoli & Cauliflower Casserole

SERVES 10–12

Ingredients

8 tbsp. butter

8 tbsp. flour

2 qts. heavy cream

1 tsp. salt

1 ½ tsp. ground white pepper

2 tsp. curry powder

florets of 2 heads broccoli

florets of 2 heads cauliflower

2 portobello mushroom caps, sliced

¾ cup panko breadcrumbs

Directions

1. Preheat the oven to 400° F/205° C

2. Place the Wonder Cooker's Roaster Pan on the stove top. Heat the butter over medium heat, whisk in the flour to make a roux, and cook for 2 mins.

3. Stir in the heavy cream, salt, ground white pepper, and curry powder. Cook until the mixture thickens slightly.

4. Add the broccoli florets, cauliflower florets, and mushrooms and then sprinkle with the panko breadcrumbs.

5. Transfer the Roaster Pan to the oven and bake at 400° F/205° C for 45 mins.

Eric's Tip: I love to get premade stuffed shells to nestle into the sauce before baking.

Spicy Creamed Corn Casserole

Ingredients

1 26-oz can condensed cream of mushroom soup

½ cup whole milk

4 15-oz cans kernel corn, drained

2 ½ cups French fried onions, divided

1 jalapeño, seeded & diced

1 red bell pepper, diced

Directions

1. Preheat the oven to 350° F/175° C.

2. Mix the soup and milk in the Wonder Cooker's Roaster Pan.

3. Stir in the corn and 1 ¼ cups fried onions.

4. Add the jalapeño and red pepper.

5. Place the Roaster Pan in the oven and bake at 350° F/175° C for 30 mins.

6. Stir and top with 1 ¼ cups fried onions.

7. Bake at 350° F/175° C for an additional 5–8 mins.

Eric's Tip: I'll turn this dish into a Maryland-style casserole by adding 8 oz fresh crab meat and 1 tbsp. crab seasoning.

Spanish Pot Roast

SERVES 4

Ingredients

Spanish Rub

2 tsp. chili powder

1 tsp. ground coriander

1 tsp. paprika

1 tsp. salt

1 tsp. ground black pepper

———

2 2 ½-lb chuck roasts

4 tbsp. canola oil, divided

3 cloves garlic, chopped

1 onion, chopped

1 shallot, chopped

1 14-oz can fire-roasted tomatoes

1 ½ cups fire-roasted corn

1 12-oz jar gravy

12 sweet baby peppers

1 ½ cups red wine

1 sprig rosemary

1 bay leaf

3 chipotle peppers, chopped

Directions

1. Preheat the oven to 350° F/175° C.

2. Combine the Spanish rub ingredients in a bowl and mix.

3. Rub the chuck roasts with the spices.

4. Place the Wonder Cooker's Roaster Pan on the stove top. Heat 2 tbsp. canola oil over medium-high heat and then brown the chuck roasts on all sides. Remove and reserve the chuck roasts.

5. Add the garlic, onion, and shallot and cook for 3–5 mins.

6. Add the chuck roasts, tomatoes, corn, gravy, baby peppers, red wine, rosemary, bay leaf, chipotle peppers, and 2 tbsp. canola oil and bring to a boil.

7. Cover the Roaster Pan with the Glass Lid, transfer to the oven, and cook at 350° F/175° C until fork tender (about 2 ½ hrs.).

Eric's Tip: I love to put this pot roast on a soft buttery brioche bun with manchego cheese and pickled red onions!

Sloppy Joe Mac & Cheese

SERVES 12

Ingredients

Cheese Sauce

2 qts. heavy cream

9 cups shredded cheddar cheese, divided

2 tbsp. cornstarch

———

2 tbsp. olive oil

6 lb ground beef

1 red bell pepper, diced

1 green pepper, diced

1 onion, diced

1 cup ketchup

1 cup tomato purée

¼ cup mustard

¼ cup Worcestershire sauce

2 tsp. onion powder

2 tsp. garlic powder

3 tbsp. chili powder

2 tbsp. paprika

1 tsp. salt

1 tsp. ground black pepper

2 lb elbow macaroni, cooked

Directions

1. Preheat the oven to 350° F/175° C.

2. Place the Wonder Cooker's Roaster Pan on the stove top. Heat the cream over medium heat.

3. Toss 8 cups cheddar cheese with the cornstarch in a bowl and then add to the Roaster Pan. Cook until the cheese melts. Remove and reserve the cheese sauce.

4. Heat the olive oil over medium heat in the Roaster Pan and then brown the ground beef.

5. Add the red bell pepper, green pepper, and onion and cook for 5 mins.

6. Add the ketchup, tomato purée, mustard, Worcestershire sauce, onion powder, garlic powder, chili powder, paprika, salt, and ground black pepper and lower the heat level to simmer for 10 mins.

7. Add the macaroni to the cheese sauce and then combine with the ground beef. Sprinkle 1 cup cheddar cheese over the top.

8. Transfer the Roaster Pan to the oven and bake at 350° F/175° C for 35–40 mins.

Eric's Tip: I also love to use this mix as a quesadilla filling served with a spicy pico de gallo.

New England Boiled Dinner

SERVES 8

Ingredients

1 12-oz beer

4 cups water

¼ cup apple cider vinegar

¼ cup brown sugar

5 lb corned beef brisket

1 head cabbage

10 baby red potatoes, small

7 carrots

Directions

1. Preheat the oven to 400° F/205° C.

2. Place the Wonder Cooker's Roaster Pan on the stove top. Bring the beer, water, apple cider vinegar, and brown sugar to a boil over high heat and then add the corned beef.

3. Cover the Roaster Pan with the Glass Lid, transfer to the oven, and bake at 400° F for 3 hrs.

4. Remove the Roaster Pan from the oven and add the cabbage, potatoes, and carrots.

5. Lower the oven to 350° F/175° C.

6. Return the Roaster Pan to the oven and bake at 350° F/175° C for 1 hr.

Eric's Tip: I always make more than I need because I'll take the leftovers the next day, give them a good chop, and make hash for breakfast – topped with sunny side up eggs, of course!

SERVES 10–12

Ingredients

Pork Rub

1 tbsp. paprika

1 tbsp. coriander

1 tbsp. sea salt

1 tbsp. ground black pepper

1 tbsp. granulated garlic

1 tbsp. minced dry onion

———

4 pork tenderloins

3 tbsp. olive oil

1 onion, diced

2 cups enchilada sauce

1 cup beef stock

3 29-oz cans black beans, drained

½ cup chopped cilantro

3 cups tortilla chips, crushed

2 cups shredded cheddar

Salsa

1 14-oz can diced fire-roasted tomatoes

2 vine ripe tomatoes, diced

½ green pepper, diced

½ jalapeño, minced

¼ red onion, diced small

3 scallions, chopped

½ tsp. sea salt

zest & juice of 1 lime

———

1 ½ cups sour cream

Pulled Pork & Black Bean Casserole

Directions

1. Combine the pork rub ingredients in a bowl and coat the tenderloins with the rub.

2. Preheat the oven to 325° F/160° C.

3. Place the Wonder Cooker's Roaster Pan on the stove top. Heat the olive oil over high heat and brown the tenderloins.

4. Add the onion, enchilada sauce, beef stock, black beans, and cilantro and bring to a boil.

5. Cover the Roaster Pan with the Glass Lid, transfer to the oven, and cook at 325° F/160° C for 2 hrs.

6. Remove from the oven, shred the meat and stir.

7. Top with the tortilla chips and cheddar cheese.

8. Return to the oven and cook at 325° F/160° C for 20 mins.

9. Combine the salsa ingredients in a bowl and mix.

10. Remove the finished casserole from the oven and top with the salsa and sour cream.

Eric's Tip: Using chuck roast in this recipe instead of pork will turn the dish into a feisty ropa vieja!

Lobster Mac & Cheese

SERVES 12

Ingredients

2 lb curly elbow macaroni

2 qts. heavy cream

1 tsp. garlic powder

1 tsp. onion powder

1 tsp. salt

1 lb cheddar, shredded

8 oz cream cheese

8 oz Gruyère cheese

10 oz grated Parmesan cheese

2 lb lobster meat, cooked

1 bunch scallions, sliced

1 cup panko breadcrumbs

Directions

1. Cook the macaroni in the Wonder Cooker's Roaster Pan according to the directions on the box. Drain and set aside when done.

2. Preheat the oven to 375° F/190° C.

3. Place the Roaster Pan on the stove top. Combine the heavy cream, garlic powder, onion powder, and salt over medium heat. Add the cream cheese, Gruyère cheese, and Parmesan cheese and cook until melted and smooth.

4. Add the cooked macaroni to the sauce and then add the lobster meat and scallions.

5. Top with the panko breadcrumbs, transfer the Roaster Pan to the oven, and bake at 375° F/190° C until the top browns (40–45 mins.).

Eric's Tip: If lobster isn't available or in the budget, try using poached shrimp or scallops instead.

Eric's Linguini & Clams

SERVES 12

Ingredients

2 sticks butter

2/3 cup olive oil

10 cloves garlic, peeled
& minced

2 onions, peeled & chopped

16 oz clam juice

2 lb linguini, broken in half

18 littleneck clams

2 32-oz cans chopped clams
in juice

2 14-oz cans diced
tomatoes

1 cup heavy cream

1 tbsp. crushed red pepper

½ cup chopped parsley

Directions

1. Place the Wonder Cooker's Roaster Pan on the stove top. Melt the butter and heat the olive oil over medium-high heat, add the garlic and onions, and cook until translucent.

2. Add the clam juice and linguini and stir well.

3. Raise the heat level to bring to a boil and stir. Add the whole clams and then cover with the Grill Pan. When the clams open, remove and reserve them.

4. Stir the linguini every few minutes until cooked al dente.

5. Add the chopped clams, tomatoes, heavy cream, crushed red pepper, and parsley. Mix to combine and continue to cook for 5 mins.

6. Top with the whole clams and serve family style.

Eric's Tip: The key to this dish is using the freshest ingredients. If clams aren't available, you can substitute mussels, shrimp, or scallops. Don't forget the crusty bread.

DESSERTS

Tangerine Cake

SERVES 16

Ingredients

2 sticks butter, room temperature

2 cups sugar

2 tbsp. tangerine zest

6 eggs

¾ cup yogurt

½ cup tangerine juice

2 tbsp. triple sec liqueur

1 tsp. vanilla extract

3 cups flour

1 tsp. baking soda

1 tsp. salt

Tangerine Icing

⅔ cup shortening

4 cups powdered sugar

zest of 2 tangerines

¼ tsp. salt

1 tbsp. tangerine juice

2 tbsp. milk

Directions

1. Preheat the oven to 350° F/175° C.

2. Combine the butter, sugar, and tangerine zest in a large bowl using an electric mixer until light and fluffy.

3. Mix the eggs, yogurt, tangerine juice, triple sec, and vanilla extract in a separate small bowl to combine. Gradually add to the large bowl to incorporate. Make sure to scrape the bowl after each addition.

4. Add flour, baking soda, and salt and mix until just combined.

5. Pour the batter into the Wonder Cooker's Roaster Pan. Place in the oven and bake at 350° F/175° C until a toothpick inserted into the center comes out clean (about 60 mins.).

6. Beat the shortening, powdered sugar, tangerine zest, and salt in a third bowl until fluffy.

7. Gradually add the tangerine juice and milk until combined to complete the icing.

8. When the cake has cooled completely, top with the icing.

Eric's Tip: I love the increasing selection of citrus at the supermarket. When I see blood oranges in season, I make this recipe. They have a nice sweet and tart flavor with an intense red color.

S'mores Cake

Ingredients

2 15 ¼-oz boxes chocolate cake mix

6 eggs

⅔ cup vegetable oil

2 cups water

2 7-oz tubs marshmallow fluff

2 12-oz containers frozen whipped topping, thawed

2 cups crushed graham crackers

2 cups mini marshmallows

2 cups chocolate chips

Directions

1. Preheat the oven to 350° F/175° C.

2. Whisk the cake mix, eggs, vegetable oil, and water in a large bowl to combine. Pour the batter into the Wonder Cooker's Roaster Pan.

3. Place the Roaster Pan in the oven and bake at 350° F/175° C for 40–45 mins.

4. Remove from the oven, let the cake cool slightly, and poke holes across the top in a grid pattern.

5. Microwave the marshmallow fluff in small increments in the microwave until the fluff reaches a spreadable consistency. Top the cake with the marshmallow fluff.

6. Top the cake with the whipped topping and sprinkle with the graham crackers.

7. Scatter the marshmallows and chocolate chips over the cake.

8. Return the Roaster Pan to the oven and bake at 350° F/175° C until the marshmallows brown.

9. Refrigerate for 30 mins. before serving.

Eric's Tip: This cake is begging for a nice, big mug of hot chocolate to help wash it down!

Spiced Apple Cake

Ingredients

4 cups thin apple slices

1 cup water

2 tbsp. maple syrup

11 tbsp. butter

2 ¼ cups sugar

¼ cup maple syrup

¼ tsp. salt

4 eggs

1 tsp. rum

5 cups all-purpose flour

2 tsp. baking soda

2 tsp. ground cinnamon

½ tsp. ground nutmeg

1 cup raisins

1 cup pecans, toasted

Directions

1. Place a saucepan on the stove top. Combine the apples, water, and maple syrup and cook over medium-high heat until the apples are soft to make the apple mixture.

2. Preheat the oven to 350° F/175° C.

3. Beat together the butter, sugar, maple syrup, and salt in the bowl of an electric mixer using the paddle attachment until fluffy.

4. While still mixing, gradually add the eggs and rum.

5. Add the flour, baking soda, cinnamon, and nutmeg and then mix until just combined.

6. Fold in the apple mixture, raisins, and pecans by hand.

7. Spread the batter in the bottom of the Wonder Cooker's Grill Pan.

8. Place the Grill Pan in the oven and bake at 350° F/175° C until a toothpick inserted into the center comes out clean (about 1–1 ½ hrs.).

Eric's Tip: Once this cake is cooled, I'll slice it thick and then prepare it French toast style topped with whipped cream for the ultimate breakfast!

Citrus Almond Cake

SERVES 8–12

Ingredients

Topping

1 cup sliced almonds

²/₃ cup sugar

½ cup unsalted butter

2 tbsp. milk

———

1 ½ cups butter, softened

²/₃ cup almond paste

2 cups sugar

1 tsp. salt

2 tsp. orange zest

8 eggs

1 tsp. vanilla extract

2 tbsp. orange juice

1 tsp. cream of tartar

3 ¹/₈ cups flour, divided

Directions

1. Place a saucepan on the stove top. Combine the topping ingredients and bring to a boil over medium-high heat.

2. Remove from the heat then set aside.

3. Preheat the oven to 350° F/175° C.

4. Beat the butter, almond paste, sugar, salt, and orange zest in the bowl of an electric mixer with the paddle attachment until light and fluffy.

5. While still mixing, gradually add the eggs, vanilla extract, and orange juice.

6. Add the cream of tartar and 3 cups flour and then mix until just combined to finish the batter.

7. Spread the batter in the Wonder Cooker's Grill Pan, sprinkle with ¹/₈ cup flour, and top with the topping.

8. Place the Grill Pan in the oven and bake at 350° F/175° C until the cake pulls away from the side of the Pan (about 1 hr.).

Eric's Tip: This after-dinner treat only needs a small nip of espresso or dark roast coffee to balance the almond sweetness.

Citrus Orange Cheesecake

SERVES 8–10

Ingredients

Vanilla Wafer Crust

1 ¼ cups vanilla wafers, crushed

¼ cup light brown sugar

½ tsp. kosher salt

½ tsp. ground cinnamon

¾ cup butter, melted

———

4 8-oz blocks cream cheese

¼ cup sour cream

1 ¼ cups sugar

zest of 2 oranges

juice of 2 oranges

Directions

1. Preheat the oven to 350° F/175° C

2. Combine the crust ingredients in a bowl and mix until a smooth paste is formed.

3. Pack the paste into the bottom of the Wonder Cooker's Roaster Pan in an even layer.

4. Place the Roaster Pan in the oven and bake at 350° F/175° C for 20 mins.

5. Remove from the oven and let cool.

6. Reduce the oven temperature to 300° F/150° C.

7. Combine the cream cheese, sour cream, and sugar in the bowl of an electric mixer. Mix on low until combined and creamy.

8. While still mixing, gradually add the eggs and then mix until fully combined.

9. Pour the cheese batter on top of the crust.

10. Cover the Roaster Pan with the Glass Lid, place in the oven, and bake at 300° F/150° C until set but still jiggly in the center (1–1 ½ hrs.).

11. Let cool completely before serving.

Eric's Tip: You can also substitute ginger snaps or chocolate wafers for the vanilla wafers to change the flavor profile!

195

Chocolate Walnut Pie

Ingredients

2 pre-prepared pie crusts

4 eggs

6 tbsp. unsalted butter, melted

1 tbsp. vanilla extract

2 cups dark brown sugar

1 cup flour

¼ cup cocoa powder

¼ tsp. salt

2 cups chopped walnuts

2 cups semisweet chocolate chips

1 cup sweetened whipped cream

Directions

1. Preheat the oven to 350° F/175° C.

2. Press the pie crusts into the Wonder Cooker's Grill Pan.

3. Beat the eggs, melted butter, vanilla extract, and dark brown sugar in a bowl using an electric mixer.

4. Add the flour, cocoa powder, and salt until just combined.

5. Fold in the walnuts and chocolate chips to complete the batter.

6. Pour the batter onto the pie crust.

7. Place the Grill Pan in the oven and bake at 350° F/175° C until the pie is golden brown (about 1–1 ¼ hrs.).

8. Top with the whipped cream.

Eric's Tip: Believe it or not, I love to eat this pie a la mode with French vanilla ice cream!

Eric's Triple Whoopie Pies

Ingredients

Cake

1 cup water

2 cups sugar

1 ¾ cups flour

¾ cup cocoa powder

1 ½ tsp. baking powder

1 tsp. salt

2 eggs

1 cup milk

½ cup vegetable oil

2 tsp. vanilla extract

Filling

1 cup milk

4 tbsp. flour

¼ tsp. salt

1 cup sugar

1 cup shortening

3 tsp. vanilla

Directions

1. Preheat the oven to 350° F/175° C.

2. Place a saucepan on the stove top. Bring the water to a boil over high heat.

3. Combine the sugar, flour, cocoa powder, baking powder, and salt in a large bowl using an electric mixer.

4. Whisk the eggs, vegetable oil, milk, and vanilla extract together in a separate small bowl until combined. Gradually add the mixture to the large bowl.

5. Slowly add the boiling water and mix until combined. Pour into the Roaster Pan.

6. Place the Roaster Pan in the oven and bake at 350° F/175° C until a toothpick inserted into the center comes out clean (about 30–35 mins.).

7. Rinse any residue out of the saucepan and return to the stove top. Whisk the milk, flour, and salt over medium heat until a thick paste forms. Let cool.

8. Beat the sugar, shortening, and vanilla together in a bowl using an electric mixer's paddle attachment for 3 mins.

9. Add the cooled paste from the saucepan and beat until light and fluffy (about 5 mins.) to complete the filling.

10. Remove the cake from the Grill Pan and cut out 12 circles with a 3-in. round cutter. Cut each circle into three even horizontal layers. Pipe the filling between each layer.

Eric's Tip: The filling is delicious as is, or it can take on different flavors. Add peanut butter, strawberry sauce, or caramel for a cool twist.

Apple Crumb Pie

Ingredients

4 pre-prepared pie crusts, cut in half

5 Granny Smith apple, peeled, cored & sliced

5 red apples, peeled, cored & sliced

1 ½ cups diced prunes

1 tbsp. cinnamon

1 cup sugar

⅓ cup flour

¼ tsp. nutmeg

juice of ½ lemon

Crumb Topping

2 cups brown sugar

1 cup flour

1 tsp. cinnamon

1 ½ sticks butter, diced

Directions

1. Preheat the oven to 350° F/175° C.

2. Place the pie crusts on the bottom and halfway up the sides of the Wonder Cooker's Roaster Pan.

3. Combine the apples, prunes, cinnamon, sugar, flour, nutmeg, and lemon juice in a bowl and toss.

4. Pour on top of the pie crust.

5. Combine the crumb topping ingredients in a separate small bowl and mix.

6. Pour the crumb topping on the pie.

7. Place the Roaster Pan in the oven and bake at 350° F/175° C until the apples are tender (about 1 ½ hrs.).

8. Let cool before cutting.

Eric's Tip: For a different twist, I'll sometimes use pears and dried apricots.

Old-Fashioned Coconut Rice Pudding

SERVES 12

Ingredients

3 13.5-oz cans coconut milk

3 cups medium-grain white rice

¾ cup sugar

2 tbsp. vanilla extract

5 tsp. ginger

3 cups heavy cream

2 eggs, beaten

½ tsp. salt

3 cups raisins

Directions

1. Preheat the oven to 375° F/190° C.

2. Place the Wonder Cooker's Roaster Pan on the stove top. Bring the coconut milk to a boil over high heat.

3. Rinse and drain the rice. Add to the boiling coconut milk. Cook for 5 mins.

4. Cover the Roaster Pan with the Glass Lid, lower the heat to low, and simmer for 20 mins.

5. Remove the Lid and stir in the sugar, vanilla extract, ginger, cream, eggs, salt, and raisins.

6. Transfer the Roaster Pan to the oven and bake at 375° F/190° C for 30–40 mins.

7. Serve in bowls.

Eric's Tip: Portion into individual ceramic or glass dishes, chill well, sprinkle the top with sugar, and brûlée with a culinary torch.

Peach Cobbler

Ingredients

4 lb frozen peaches, thawed

1 tbsp. cinnamon

¾ cup sugar

Cobbler Topping

1 ½ cups flour

1 ¼ cups almond flour

¾ cup coconut oil

1 tsp. almond extract

2 tsp. baking powder

1 cup buttermilk

1 cup sliced almonds

½ cup brown sugar

Directions

1. Preheat the oven 350° F/175° C.

2. Place the Wonder Cooker's Roaster Pan on the stove top. Combine the peaches, cinnamon, and sugar and bring to a boil over high heat for 4 mins.

3. Combine the flour, almond flour, coconut oil, almond extract, baking powder, and buttermilk in a bowl to make the cobbler topping.

4. Sprinkle the topping, almonds, and brown sugar on the peaches.

5. Transfer the Roaster Pan to the oven and bake at 350° F/175° C until golden brown (about 30 mins.).

Eric's Tip: I love to use frozen mango in this cobbler as well!

Blueberry Buckle

Ingredients

Streusel Topping

1 cup sugar

²/₃ cup flour

1 tsp. ground cinnamon

½ cup butter

——

½ cup butter, softened

1 ½ cup brown sugar

1 tsp. salt

zest of ½ lemon

2 eggs

1 cup milk, room temperature

1 ¹/₃ tbsp. baking powder

4 ¹/₈ cups flour, divided

3 cups blueberries

2 tbsp. flour

Directions

1. Preheat the oven to 350° F/175° C.

2. Add the streusel topping ingredients to a bowl and mix until combined. Place the bowl in the refrigerator to firm up.

3. Beat the butter, brown sugar, salt, and lemon zest in the bowl of an electric mixer using the paddle attachment until light and fluffy.

4. While still mixing, gradually add the eggs and milk.

5. Add the baking powder and 4 cups flour and then mix until just combined.

6. Toss the blueberries with ¹/₈ cup flour and then fold them into the batter by hand.

7. Spread the batter in the bottom of the Wonder Cooker's Grill Pan in an even layer. Sprinkle the streusel topping on top of the batter.

8. Place the Grill Pan in the oven and bake at 350° F/175° C until a toothpick inserted into the center comes out clean (about 1 hr.).

Eric's Tip: Try using local orchard apples or pears when they are in season. Just peel, sauté, cool, and chop.

Strawberry Rhubarb Crisp

SERVES 8

Ingredients

5 stalks rhubarb, diced

3 lb strawberries, sliced

1 tsp. cinnamon

zest & juice of ½ lemon

⅓ cup sugar

Crisp Topping

1 stick butter

½ cup flour

1 ½ cups brown sugar

1 cup granola

Directions

1. Preheat the oven to 350° F/175° C.

2. Combine the rhubarb, strawberries, cinnamon, lemon juice, lemon zest, and sugar in a bowl.

3. Pour the mixture into the Wonder Cooker's Grill Pan.

4. Place the Grill Pan in the oven and bake at 350° F/175° C for 20 mins.

5. Combine the crisp topping ingredients in a separate bowl.

6. Remove the Grill Pan from the oven. Pour the topping over the fruit.

7. Return to the oven and bake at 350° F/175° C until golden brown (about 35 mins.).

Eric's Tip: Rhubarb has such a unique flavor, but if you can't find it, use equal parts of tart apples, like Granny Smith apples.

Chocolate Peanut Butter Cake

SERVES 8–12

Ingredients

2 cups water

1 cup peanut butter

4 cups sugar

3 ½ cups flour

1 ½ cups cocoa

3 tsp. baking powder

3 tsp. baking soda

2 tsp. salt

4 eggs

1 cup vegetable oil

2 cups milk

4 tsp. vanilla extract

Peanut Butter Frosting

1 cup creamy peanut butter

1 ¼ sticks unsalted butter, softened & cut into cubes

2 cups powdered sugar

2 tsp. vanilla extract

¼ tsp. salt

2 tbsp. heavy cream

2 cups peanut butter candy

chocolate syrup, for topping

Directions

1. Preheat the oven to 350° F/175° C.

2. Place a saucepan on the stove top. Bring the water to a boil, add the peanut butter, and stir until dissolved.

3. Combine the sugar, flour, cocoa, baking powder, baking soda, and salt in a large bowl using an electric mixer.

4. Whisk the eggs, vegetable oil, milk, and vanilla extract together in a separate small bowl. Gradually add to the large bowl until combined.

5. Add the dissolved peanut butter to the large bowl and mix until combined.

6. Pour the batter into the Roaster Pan. Place in the oven and bake at 350° F/175° C until a toothpick inserted into the center comes out clean (about 45 mins.).

7. Combine the peanut butter and butter in a bowl using an electric mixer to begin making the peanut butter frosting.

8. Add the powdered sugar, vanilla extract, and salt and then beat until light and fluffy.

9. Gradually beat in the cream.

10. When the cake is cooled, top with the peanut butter frosting, peanut butter candy, and chocolate syrup.

Eric's Tip: Try using almond butter or chocolate hazelnut spread in the frosting instead of peanut butter.

Index

M

N

O

P

Z